Beyond the Pulpit

Beyond the Pulpit

✦

A Journey to the World to Heal the Broken Heart

Dr. Arthur A. Rouner, Jr.

iUniverse, Inc.

New York Lincoln Shanghai

Beyond the Pulpit
A Journey to the World to Heal the Broken Heart

iUniverse, Inc.

For information address:
iUniverse, Inc.
2021 Pine Lake Road, Suite 100
Lincoln, NE 68512
www.iuniverse.com

ISBN: 0-595-30061-8

Printed in the United States of America

Contents

Preface

✦

A New Way of Mission

Churches of the "mainline" in America were not unfamiliar with mission. Many had noble traditions of mission with names of heroes all their own.

The church I served was of the Congregational order. We were descended from Pilgrims and Puritans, who came to America seeking freedom for their life in local congregations from the oppression of the State Church in England, that enjoyed the power of bishops and sheriffs to force local churches to follow the wishes of the State's church.

These churches fashioned a free way in the New World that was ordered by the people of the local congregations themselves. As their life began on the edge of the wilderness on the shores of what was to become Massachusetts, their sense of mission came from the very heart of their congregational life.

They were there to influence the society that grew up around them. They cared about each other. Half of the company died that first winter in Plymouth Plantation. They had to nurse, feed, and bury each other.

Surrounding them were the Indian people of the Wampanoag tribe. One of them, Squanto, early befriended them, teaching the settlers how to plant corn. Their survival that first winter was greatly due to the help of the Indian people. Over time there was intermarriage with the Indians. There was also a great desire to share with the Indian people their deep belief in the God whose love had sent Jesus into the world to save all people.

An early hero of this Congregational Way was John Eliot, pastor to the Puritan Congregation in Roxbury, on the edge of the settlement at Boston, who mounted his horse each Sunday afternoon after church, and rode out into the forests, meeting the Indian people and gathering them together to hear about Jesus. They Indians actually formed themselves into villages that centered in those teaching times.

To help them study and grow in this Christian faith, John Eliot patiently learned the sounds of their spoken language, and from that exercise slowly fashioned and gave to them a written language in the form of the Scriptures. This was the *Algonquin Bible*, America's earliest and most valuable book, which is now carefully kept and treasured in the Boston Public Library.

Another Congregational hero of mission was Jonathan Edwards, pastor to the Congregational Church in Northampton, Massachusetts, nearly a century later. His preaching helped to bring about the Great Awakening of the 1740's, even though its enthusiasm…and his own attempts to exercise discipline among his people…brought his ministry to an end in Northampton.

What did he do then? He went to the Indians of western Massachusetts, where he not only preached to them, but wrote there some of his most thoughtful and influential treatises.

So, there was a missionary spirit in those first centuries of the "Congregational Way" in America. The Puritans, who came to Boston soon after the Pilgrims…who had preceded them in Plymouth…spoke of this sense of having "an errand into the wilderness." They saw themselves as messengers to take good news into the wilderness places of this immense continent.

They wanted to influence their communities. They wanted to establish a society built on the Biblical principles of a community caring for each other, of justice and love, and of society being fair and equitable. Clearly, they did not always succeed in that, but they fashioned a set of community, commonwealth, and ultimately country concerns that were picked up by the revolutionary generation that followed them in the latter 1700's.

That same spirit lived into the next century when a group of students at Williams College in western Massachusetts, had a thunderstorm experience later known as the Haystack Prayer Meeting. This re-ignited a missionary fervor that began in the second decade of the 1800's, calling young men and their families to go literally to the ends of the world to tell the story of Jesus.

They went first to Burma, becoming "Baptists" on shipboard, and then went to the Hawaiian Islands. Thus was American's first Board of Missions formed: "The American Board of Commissioners for Foreign Missions."

Later generations gave us Frank Laubach and his mission to the Philippines. The Methodists, with their spirit of frontier ministry in America, were also to have their E. Stanley Jones and his mission to India.

The 20th century, building on a real tradition among the Protestant churches, brought formal denominational mission boards, with chosen trained missionaries sent out "under the board." Missionaries were paid by the national boards, and their work was directed by them.

Gradually, the call to evangelize faded in those traditions, with a philosophy rising of "partnerships" with the missions that had already been established. It was a right spirit of cooperating with those to whom western Christians had taken the Gospel, but more and more it became a movement centered in plans and strategies made by national bodies. The obligation then became for local churches to do their part by providing the funds with which the national board would direct the denomination's missionary enterprise.

Just as the great ecumenical fervor of the 1940's, 50's, and 60's went aground on the assumption that all church traditions would unite into one great organization...the better with which to influence the world...the missionary movement more and more took away the missionary thrust and spirit from local churches. This left local churches simply the funding bodies of missions.

Rebellion was in the air all across American society in the 1960's, and so also with the churches. Gradually local churches claimed not only independence for themselves, but also independence for their own sense of mission. "Why send money to headquarters for someone else to be a missionary? Why not be missionaries ourselves, and we will go across the land and world to proclaim the gospel?"

Thus in the 1960's, the idea of mission independence began to change first toward designating their own missionaries and support for them, and within the next decades, toward the sending out of groups. First they sent young people, and then adults, to serve in "short-term" missions. They would go where they could to build schools or other facilities in needy parts of America, but more and more, they went to Mexico, Haiti, Africa, or South America.

It was at the very threshold of this idea...this "new thing"...that the call came to a group of churches in the unlikely suburb of Edina, Minnesota, to go to the world to do something they could do together...that is, to *feed the hungry*. Their own theological differences would have precluded their doing a classical Gospel proclamation and teaching mission, but Catholics, fundamental Baptists, evangelical Congregationalists and Presbyterians, and traditional Lutherans could all get together on the cause of feeding the hungry.

They *could* do the work of Christian compassion, and that they discovered that the Gospel was proclaimed. It was the Gospel of love, the witness of humble service...of Christians of differing traditions serving together in the Name of Jesus.

Something quite new in missions was happening here. World Vision itself had never before done anything like this. The organization had never taken a group of Americans on a journey anywhere across the world just to see and be moved to do something about the most aching needs of the "Two-Thirds World."

So the journey to Africa was a new adventure for that great Christian non-denominational agency, and certainly a new adventure for those local congregations. The latter were breaking away from their own denominational pattern without even realizing it. They would be challenged, viewed as renegades by those denominations, but it was too heady an experience to turn back...these local churches had embarked on their high adventure of going out to the world together.

Introduction

❖

The Ending of a Ministry

In the eyes of the contemporary world, with its whole new set of prejudices springing from "modernity," much of what Christians do and what they believe is viewed as monumental arrogance. "Who are these Christians anyway, who think the only way to God is through Jesus, that Nobody from Nazareth? Who are these people who think they have the answer...in faith...for this America and this world...a world that doesn't *want* faith? Who are these people who want to save America, and save the world?"

Sometimes being a Christian, particularly as a pastor of a flock, or as a missionary to the needs of some isolated people in a far country, *feels* like arrogance.

To go off to Rwanda just two years after the terrible genocide in that land, and to think you are going to bring reconciliation to people who have hated and killed each other's family members...and who now deeply fear each other...seems like madness...the madness of a Don Quixote, galloping off in his tin hat with his bent lance to "tilt at windmills," strangely imagining them to be enemy giants or dragons.

The world looks on and laughs. It tends to diminish such purposes and escapades as not only ridiculous, but palpably impossible. That judgment is largely based one's own personal experience of often having at least one non-reconciled relationship in his or her life. People cannot seem to get past those inner walls of protection in their lives, so to them it is inconceivable that anyone as inexperienced and ordinary as themselves could possibly go off and attempt...much less succeed...in bringing off a coming-together of two tribes of peoples who have generations of hurt between them...and recently, one of the most appalling examples of genocidal killing between them that this world has ever known.

You even wonder what the Tutsis and Hutus themselves must think. Maybe it's something such as, "Paul I know, and Jesus I know...but who are *you*?"

As my tenth year "beyond the pulpit" comes to a close, I look back amazed at what has happened...*No!* At what *God has wrought.*

How could I have been, on a damp November day, in the northern Rwanda town of Byumba, in a crowded little room in the World Vision Center, on what was almost a mountaintop? We were nearly within sight of Uganda, as we met with fifteen pastors who represented a dozen different religious traditions…including the Roman Catholic. As we quietly talked, wept, and prayed, we carried the message that we had come from the Church of the *world*, to stand with them as brothers and sisters. After three hours they begged, "Stay with us. Stay two weeks, and if not that, stay two days…or at least two more hours! Talk to us. Be with us!"

They were a broken community, and they were puzzled pastors. It was Hutu country, and much killing had happened in the Byumba region. After all, it was from the north, across that blue border that could almost be seen in the distance, that the Tutsi rebel army, having staged mysteriously in Uganda, had come pouring down to ignite the civil war that triggered the fear-filled Hutu government in those awful days of April 1994, sending out the message across that tiny land: "The Tutsi's are coming. You must kill all Tutsis…your neighbors, your wife, your husband, your colleagues. If you do not kill them, they will kill you!"

And so it had begun, there in the north, and the Church, in a land approximately 90% Christian, did not stand. It did not shout, "No! This shall not be!" Some Christian leaders cried out and they were killed. Some fled in fear. Some turned away. Some did the killing themselves, or permitted or allowed it to be done.

So the Church had not stopped the carnage, but here they were, trying to "do Church," trying to rally the people and help them *be* the Church again. "We don't know what to do," they confessed. "Help us understand and go forward. Our people have so little, they are so poor, and that keeps them from doing the Gospel work of reconciliation!"

Sensing this pastor was tempted to set us up for financial help, I said, "I came from a large church that I served for many years that was *not* poor, that had so much that it, too, could not break free to seek reconciliation, and be healed."

I have thought much about that odd history of my own life, as our reconciliation team of three worked through that remarkable year of 1996-97. We journeyed three times to Rwanda, meeting many people, making many friends, leading seven healing retreats "At the Foot of the Cross"…first, in March, with twelve other pastors, then with leaders of Youth for Christ, with two local churches and their leaders, with woman leaders representing each of the twelve prefectures of Rwanda, and perhaps most dramatically, with thirty of the staff of the Protestant Council of Rwanda (PCR).

Before our eyes we watched the dominating, authoritarian Secretary General of the PCR…a man shot through with grief and trauma following the murder of his wife and six children (including his 2 1/2 month old baby)…go to his knees in prayer and confession, and then rise suddenly…so freed in healing that my dear wife Molly could only exclaim, "I saw Satan fall like lightening from heaven!"

Then there was his dysfunctional, antagonistic, hurt office staff…suddenly broken down and broken open…asking forgiveness, confessing sin, praying, hugging each other, and going from tears to singing, dancing, and laughing. Strange, wonderful "joy in the morning" came with a spiritual power we could not miss.

Our small team had simply come…so far…to be with them in love, reminding them of the Cross and the shed blood of Jesus, entering into this deeply emotional experience with them…of remembering, confessing, and forgiving. Miraculously, reconciliation just *happened*. By God's grace it happened.

Indeed, that day was also my birthday. I was 68 years old, and in the midst of all their emotion, these people chose to celebrate it with "Grandpa."

What would it all mean…this remarkable ministry, at the foot of the cross, 10,000 miles from home, in our old age? As one of our own children had said, only a few weeks before we returned to Rwanda, "You could be in Mexico, lying on a beach in the sun, taking a well-deserved rest." My determined, sweet wife's response had been, "But that's not the way I want to live my life."

Rwanda had been a deep experience for all three of us on our team of two old white folks from middle America, and Tekle Selassie, our Ethiopian colleague with fifteen years of country directorship experience with World Vision in Africa.

The previous March, Tekle had come back late from Rwanda with a swelling in his neck and a respiratory problem he could not shake. His doctor had immediately asked, "Have you been in a place where you may have experienced trauma?"

"Well, yes, I have been sitting and listening to some of the most horrendous human experiences of killing and fear I could ever imagine," Tekle responded.

"There you are," the doctor answered.

Then Molly had an experience in early April of speaking to a circle of church women…her dear friends…about Rwanda, and about her experiences and work there. Something happened at that innocent luncheon of faithful women who had gathered to hear their Christian friend bare her heart about an experience that had been so deep in her life.

Her friends told me later that at one point, Molly had said with tears, "I just can't get beyond Rwanda!" They had responded, "Molly, your talk was so vivid. You actually took us with you to Rwanda…but then you seemed to have trouble coming back."

She had been somewhat confused as she finished her story. Her friends of so many years then said, "That was wonderful Molly. Now, tell us about your children," but frighteningly, Molly could not remember their names. Her friends knew, and she knew, that something strange had happened. Suddenly, she could not remember the talk she had given, or why she had come. The women phoned me and put my wife on the line, and Molly said, "We're having some confusion here. There's a lot I can't remember. I was telling the circle about Rwanda, and suddenly I was confused."

We headed for the hospital emergency room. "Now where are we going?" she repeated. "Did I give a talk? What did I say? Did I tell them any dirty stories?"

"Molly, don't worry." I reassured her. "You don't even know any dirty stories!"

While she had trouble remembering, Molly's doctors found no evidence of stroke or heart complication. There were no symptoms but this strange loss of memory relating to her deep experience of Rwanda.

"Transient Global Amnesia" had taken her memory for six hours. There were no indications that it would likely return, the doctors said from their experience. They were loath to speculate about the cause of the sudden memory loss, however, hoping it would not be replayed.

It was clear that our team's concerns had been about the wrong kinds of dangers…We had thought about airplanes, small and big, and dark, shadowed roadways where mines and militia lurked…rather than about the great Enemy who had turned Rwanda into a killing field by means of hate that could not be stopped. He held a whole nation in the thrall of fear and grief…Why would He let anyone come with a message of love to heal the land over which He still held such control?

It was warfare of the spirit…a new kind of danger to us. Suddenly we knew that we must be prepared and protected by corresponding spiritual power…"the whole armor of God"…which could be ours only by prayer.

What had we fallen into? What was this ministry God had given us? What were to be the new dangers, the new dimensions, of this journey out across the world, into a "parish" that now was everywhere?

The challenge was dramatic. The possibilities seemed suddenly very real. We were in the midst of a year more intense…and probably deeper…and quite possibly more profound and close to the heart of the Gospel, than anything we had yet experienced.

And yet, all that we had learned and experienced in forty years of pastoral ministry would be useful in this new work. We knew that all we had known and loved so deeply for all those years of service in parish ministry would somehow be fully used in the new ministry of *reconciliation*, the ministry of healing the broken heart…of mending the deepest divisions between people, and between them and God.

I began to see that I had been prepared, and that all those years I had loved of parish work were not wasted. Even the final two to three years of the ending of that long ministry…full of its many kinds of misunderstandings, power struggling, betrayal, and even the experience of my own heart breaking…would all be used for good.

So much good had been done in those 32 years of ministry. There had been many Sundays of high worship…sermons of the heart poured out…many people seen and loved wholeheartedly in their pain…many hospital bedsides visited and cemeteries seen…many hands held and prayers lifted that only God knows. There had been many young people taught the faith, and many lonely collegians personally visited on their college campuses. So many courses had been taught, and visions had been lifted up and fulfilled. There had been so many journeys out with so many people. There had been such high adventure…*so* much…but which was, in the end, not enough.

A predatory spirit can overtake a Christian company when its people are not alert. Schemes for power can take the opportunity to unfold, and the destruction they wreak…and the fragile web of gossamer relations of a church family's life they shred and break…are simply not understood. It takes only a handful of people to have their way through the most simple and elemental means…i.e. through *talk*, as an angry murmur underlying the surface of a great church's life…to bring a ministry down.

This results in not simply bringing down a professional minister's ministry…but the ministries of hundreds of people who are part of that ministry…who have cared deeply and who have both followed and led. *Their* service to Christ is assaulted. *Their* beliefs in themselves and their church, and in the good faith of their leader whom they saw as anointed, is challenged…if not completely shattered.

How did it go so wrong for me at Colonial Church? Who knows? Clearly, as Bob Dylan so arrestingly sang, "the times they [were] a-changin'."

A new morality truly had overtaken America's thoughts, beliefs, and life-style. It had overtaken the Church's life-style…even that of the so-called evangelical Church.

Self, for three decades, had been lifted high. Serving oneself had become the moral purpose of many an American. The Sexual Revolution ushered that in. People wanted to have sexual freedom, but in order to do so that meant that the old restraints…the old "order"…had to be set aside. Morals of the past that had come from the codes of Scripture, and from the God of the Bible, were the source of those restraints. For the self to have complete freedom, the responsibilities that had been lain on community, Church, family, and marriage by God, must somehow be done away.

The 60's, 70's and 80's were days of "enlightenment" rationality gone large…building the case for the self, establishing in America *tolerance* as the greatest virtue, and *judgment* as the most wicked sin. So a church…however wonderful…and a pulpit…however irenic, articulate, and even loving…that dared to tell the truth about Self vs. God…began to be perceived to have moved far to the right. Calling upon community and individuals to "humble themselves beneath the mighty hand of God," and to stand against not only sexual excesses, but ethical distortions, financial greed, and the life-style liberties of these years, the leadership of the Church seemed to have become intolerant of the easy compromises that were more and more characterizing American life.

The media depicted many unattractive models of not only overzealous ministry, but also of financially, sexually, and personally "fallen" ministries. Who was to say that even Colonial's minister and ministry…so long-loved, and seemingly so faithful and strong…wasn't a ministry gone wrong? Was it a ministry that cared *too* much about principle and morality? Was it a ministry that did not defend the growing American enchantment with "the market" that measured success by achievement, a ministry that did not seem to honor enough how good people really were?

The "everything goes" mentality, which had come to be taught in our highly "psychologized" society, came to mean, in fact, that no criticism could be given, especially if it could be seen as personal. The whole society was ready to strike back if you…as the teen-age rap ethos had it, "disrespect me!"

In the late 80's and the early 90's, American church life…in its official denominational leadership…was enchanted with growth and with "big"…"big church," "big minister," "big program," "big budget." If you did anything to risk that...even if your leadership had been a significant factor in creating the growth...you very quickly became at least a pariah, if not an enemy.

If you had led the church in the risky things that lead to sacrifice and service...such as going into the inner city to support new ministries, to reach out to delinquent girls to establish an inter-racial nursery, to establish halfway houses for ex-prisoners, or to help found street academies...some would say that you were not willing to stay safe in the suburbs and let the Church of the suburbs ignore the dying poor. These commentators may then store up resentment in their hearts against you.

Or if, as the church grew, you used your influence to support its moving to a new place, and building a new meeting house across the town at a cost of three to four million dollars, some would remember that too, and say to you fifteen years later, "Yes, I have been angry with you ever since you led the church to move and build a new building. I knew then that you were going in a different direction from me. And I've resented that you have kept me from major leadership in the church too!" Resentment had been cherished for fifteen years, and a perception had been nourished that one's personal power was being thwarted. How human we are...even within the Church of Christ.

If your life had been touched twenty years before by the hand of God, and His Spirit had descended upon you...and you thereafter labored quietly to lift up and teach those truths to a congregation still growing, that too might be well chalked up by some as embarrassing, too personal, and too sensational to be trusted or continued. Even if in the latter days you had tried more carefully to fold a sense of the Spirit's leading and love into the church's public worship and governance life, you risked criticism.

If, after the new church had been built, and the call had come to go ecumenically with ministers and people from five other neighboring churches to the dying and starving in Africa...and you raised in your own church $150,000 for that human need so far away, it became easy for some to say, "You don't really love us any more. You care more about the Africans than you do for us."

In fact, if they think you do too much or too many things in worship, pastoral caring, weddings, and funerals...these things you love and were trained to do...a case could be made that you didn't share enough with other staff, or that you weren't democratic enough.

By the time in the early 90's, when a gay/lesbian church was being wooed for membership in your denominational association, and you and your church council had both stood in opposition to such a membership...on the grounds that "church" is about *Christ* instead of about sexual lifestyles...and that homosexuals should be in *all* of our churches, struggling with the rest of us to find wholeness and forgiveness in our lives…and you are interviewed by the press, and the issue goes public…more than a few people could say, "Aha! At last he has gone too far. This intolerant, judgmental position shows that he has moved too far to the right. He no longer speaks for the "moderate" people of the church. He has overstepped this time. This ministry must end."

At Colonial, as the little clusters connected, and conversations spread in the hallways, exaggerations went unchallenged, and things that were not true were laid forth as if they were. For some it became simply a matter of time…How soon and in what way could the deed be done? Who would organize and orchestrate the departure?

People do not like to be honest about such things. Rarely are they forthright. They do not want to sit down and negotiate on the basis of truth. What Christians in the churches seem to prefer is to slowly erode, undercut, undermine, and diminish. They raise questions about the leader, about the motives of his service, and try to suggest that even the good things have been done for the wrong reason.

Most particularly, they will set up forums for criticism, gathering people who will make complaints…so the person being ousted will take all of the responsibility himself for the things which are said to be "floundering." They will make attempts to so undercut the subject's self-confidence that he will take guilt upon himself, and he will, as psychologist M. Scott Peck has suggested, believe the lie and depart from the game.

So it was with me…in one of the great churches of American parish church life. Worship, service, mission, and heart and spirit, doesn't get any better than they did in Colonial Church, but even there, friends turned violent and away. People I had loved and served many years…those whom with I'd given and even helped…led the way in making it happen.

First, there were several distinct waves of undermining. Each had a distinct leader and each had a clear agenda.

Even after the leaders had my resignation, one leader worked to undercut our ministry enough so that I would leave before the agreed-upon date of my departure. Meetings were called that included even my own staff, where each one was asked, "Do you believe Arthur is able to survive the time here until his agreed date of departure?" The staff…human as they were…said that I could not. It also became known to me that three different staff members had been encouraged at different times by the lay leaders of the church to think that each of them was to become the new leader of the church after my departure.

So, the wounds were deep from the ending of those thirty-two years of ministry. Strangely, however, the work of preparation had already been done to prepare my wife and me for a ministry of bringing people together across lines of hurt and hate. Parish ministry ended, while eventually a new ministry...stronger and deeper than ever...was being forged for us.

This book is about that developing, reconciling ministry...across the world.

1

The Sending of a Minister

With God, the "ending of a ministry" seems often to preclude preparation for the "sending of a minister."

In the closing painful days of my ministry among the people I loved in the parish church that had been essentially my life's work, one of the lay leaders, prepared to defend me and keep me alive in that ministry of so many years, insisted on pursuing the question, "Do you have a call to a ministry other than Colonial?"

Huge church meetings had gathered around the issue of whether my offer to resign my ministry there, in the interest of bringing about reconciliation within the body of that great church, acknowledged that I had the right to the continuing leadership of the church because God had not withdrawn His Call to me or His anointing of my life for that ministry.

His question was a delicate one. I, in fact, had no sense that God was calling me to any other ministry "out there," or that somehow "one clear call" had come that I must now follow. I had no awareness of something different, bigger, or smaller to which I must go, and therefore must *leave* The Colonial Church of Edina, Minnesota.

However, I honestly felt that it was right for me to leave. I had said publicly that I would submit my resignation, effective September 1, 1994, if God could use it for the healing of this church that I loved.

I would, by that date, be old enough to go. Not only would there be for me a nice symbolism in leaving on the anniversary of the day I had arrived at Colonial 32 years before, as well as of the day I had begun my life in the parish ministry 40 years before, but I would also by then be 65 years of age. If I were to be turned out…by their decision or mine…I would not go on to nothing. There would be the annuity that the denomination offered, and there would be the Social Security the country offered.

And, I would not go easily into that good night. I might not rage against the dark, but I would go with what grace and dignity God would give me, and I would go on a schedule I believed that He would provide.

They would need to live with me a year. We would have to face each other, and work together for the common good of the church we both loved. I would concede the long-held dream of serving Colonial to the year 2000, and celebrating the 50th year of the Church, whose pastor I had been for 32 of those years, and celebrating…as a parish minister…the 2000th year of Christianity in the world. The church, or those within it also wished my demise, would have their hopes fulfilled to have me gone, but they would not have their way immediately. I believed that my offer was right, and that to stay longer, or to insist on staying, was probably untenable. So, while my answer to my friend had to be, "I have no other call," it still could not be said that leaving now was not God's plan.

How Do You See the Plan?

In that painful period of the early winter of 1993, I simply could not see the plan. The things of destruction that had been happening in that great church's life were surely not the work of God, but they were more likely the work of God's enemy, the Evil One.

Friends had turned away. Some seemed to want a power they felt they had not previously had. Only later did I realize that the names of three others on the staff would be put forward as my successors. For some potential kingmakers in the church, there was no time to lose. That in itself would make that final year from June of 1993 to June of 1994, painful indeed.

The spring held agonizing church meetings. Enough people who wanted to make a point had withheld their pledges, that we would be $300,000 short of our $2,000,000 budget. This ultimately translated into a downsizing of staff. By June, three of us on the professional staff would be on our way out, and before many months, a total of ten staff members would lose their jobs.

An officer of the church made every effort to have me leave long before the date at which I had offered to go. As it turned out, he had his own candidate for my position.

The struggles of that strange year were not only over church governance, but also over what kind of music would characterize our worship. This issue resulted in a gifted young Music Director being nearly destroyed. On top of that, a scandal of sexual assault emerged from the past surrounding another member of the staff.

It was a year of attempting to make personal peace with certain individuals and reconciliation within the body of the church. Church meetings were held to appoint search committees for an Interim Senior Minister, as well as for a permanent Senior Minister. Misunderstanding and misperception seemed to be everywhere.

What, in all of this, was the plan…God's plan?

Mercifully, something began among friends within the flock. As the church began to deal with what departure "package" would be given this minister who had served them so long, a plan ultimately was put into place for friends to provide a fund to approach what the church might have officially done. As this fund began to be solicited in the spring of 1994, a wonderful group of friends, who referred to themselves as the "Dream Team," gathered in a series of meetings to plan what eventually would be called "The Rouner Center for Missions and Ministry."

They were a "dream team" because they dreamed, with Molly and me, of what a ministry might be, beyond Colonial, with elements in the realm of missions that some had dreamed of for Colonial itself. They saw a center through which mission could continue to go out to the world, and through which a personal pastoral ministry could still be carried on. Through this center, television ministry could have a new life, and some of the very things that critics within the church had wanted to end, could have new lives outside and beyond the church. It was the bare beginning of "a plan."

A place for this center would be provided in the office of a leader in the church…two rooms in an office building that was central, visible, and accessible. The "price was right" because the space was free. For three years this "center"…out of which ministry could proceed…was there as an identifiable "place" for me to be.

Our theme was the American pilgrim sense of "The Journey," not only a sense of Israel's wandering out across the world, but very much the sense of spiritual pilgrimage, the inner journey of the heart as it seeks to find meaning. This soon picked up on the idea of "The Journey" which had become the spirit of Colonial Church's life…and my life: As pilgrim Christians, we were always in process, always on a journey…most particularly on a journey with Jesus on which we see the world of the poor to whom He introduces us. Through the journey we also see for ourselves our own personal walk with Him, and we discover ourselves in new ways as belonging to Him.

The logo of this new ministry was the figure of a man walking…out into the world…alone. It seemed to symbolize the change in my own life. For me now, as for John Wesley of 250 years before, "The World [was] My Parish." Behind is left the whole settled life of parish ministry with its daily huge and unrelenting tasks. Ahead is the unknown world…the world of far places, of new friends and adventures, and the world's need.

The new Center for Missions and Ministry would call people to "go out." It would call them to the world. It would *take* them to the world.

As we had already been taking people from our church's life to be bridges of love from middle America to the heart of Africa, and also on "Journeys of Hope Along the Trail of Tears" to the Indian reservations of the west, and then on journeys into the Minnesota wilderness to paddle and portage and become close to God, our Center now would specialize in journeys of mission that would touch other people and help them, but which could also dramatically change the lives of travelers.

We would accompany teams of young businessmen to Africa, and Gospel crusades to India. We would venture even to old and New England, the places of the first travelers of our Pilgrim Puritan Congregational heritage. We would minister to the hurt ministers we knew…the "wounded healers" of America, and would love and help restore them.

We would preach and teach about the Congregational Way, and about the life of Jesus. We would meet folks for series of teachings about the *Bible*. We would welcome them for worship in our homes a few times a year. We would send them a newsletter, *The Journey Out,* to encourage them and to inform them of our work. We would continue a television presence with a Monday evening program called *There's More to Life,* and offer a message on our daily Faith Line. We would send out audiotapes of sermons, and videotapes of our cable program, and continue to write books. We would be a *presence* in the community, and in the world, for Jesus. Our style, our spirit, would be different. There would be no "big sell," but instead an honest introduction of Jesus around the substantiation of life. We would even see people privately over coffee at local coffee shops. We weren't giving up on caring, because this would be, in America and across the world, a "ministry of presence!" We would "be there" in as many ways as we could.

We weren't, however, a church. What were we? Were we just a ministry…of an old man who didn't want to give up his ministry? Or were we something new…the ministry of an institution that would have a staff? Would we gather volunteers? Recruit people? Would we begin to be our own "movement," with certain services, qualities, and purposes that would characterize our life?

Surely, we would do *good*. Surely we would help people grow and deepen in their own lives, but initially, even members of the staff asked, "Is the Rouner Center simply *Arthur*...or is it something more?

Initially it was not clear. Those early years were a groping forward. In the first year we accepted every invitation to serve, just to see where it would lead.

But we were always putting something together as we endeavored to help restore lives, relationships, and ministries that were damaged or broken. We were praying, teaching, and leading toward unity.

Finally, after eight years, it became clear that we were about *reconciliation*, about breaking down the "middle wall of partition" that separates people from each other; we were about the healing of hate, hurt, and residual anger. *Our work would be about bringing people home to God and home to each other.*

In our third year, World Vision proposed a partnership with us to do the work of healing and reconciliation in the African nations of Rwanda and Burundi. We would form a team of an old white guy who had loved Africa for fifteen years, and who had served Africa through funding the end of starvation and the building up of the resources of that land...all the while leading a middle American parish church in its life at home...and a younger Ethiopian man with fifteen years experience as a Country Director for World Vision in Africa. Added to that team would be an elderly white woman with great wisdom and a lifetime of teaching, non-profit management, and retreat leadership experience.

They would go to Rwanda. They would do retreats there that began to bring miraculous healing results. They would take their retreat ministry to Burundi. They would apply it to Rwandan students at Daystar University in Nairobi, who at first could hardly be in the same room with each other, much less pray together, after the horrors of the genocide back home had filled them with such deep fear and suspicion.

There it was, as clear as could be: The Center's mission already was reconciliation! Reconciliation was its *focus*. Reconciliation was its *heart*. Reconciliation was the deepest ministry of what was now renamed *The Pilgrim Center for Reconciliation.*

In going to the depths of people's deeply painful lives filled in far-off Rwanda, it had become very clear that here, amazingly, was a "call" on my life, and it was different and deeper than anything I had been given before...even in those wonderful years of parish ministry. It is not that my previous ministry was less important, or was or no longer desired or useful. It is simply that helping God heal the hurt and hate in a human heart is the deepest and maybe the most important work for a minister...or a ministry...to do. My brother, a theological professor, said, "It's not that parish ministry wasn't deep or wonderful. It's that you are going from that life to the most important work you've ever done…the crown of your whole ministry."

Here, surely, was "the call" for which my friend had looked…not obviously, suddenly, or dramatically seen by me. But this was clearly the call to my wife and me as a whole new ministry together. It was the new call that would use everything we had ever learned.

One ministry ended…but miraculously and wonderfully…a new ministry emerged. A door closed in great pain, but a window opened with a wonderful exhilaration into a time of remarkable new possibilities.

2

Gifts: The Wisdom of the Years

One of the wonders of life with God, the life of faith, is that if we let Him, God will keep teaching us until we die.

My own "post-parish" life could have been filled with much that I love…set primarily in the context of the dream of so many of us Americans have of the life of ease called "retirement." The marvel, however, is that instead God is filling these years with so many things to learn about, and with new knowledge. In some ways, best of all, He is filling them with new insights about all of life and about the past…my own, and the world's. I am learning about God Himself, about the Church, about people, and about the way of faith.

It could have been all over with the ending of the 32 years of parish ministry within a growing congregation of people dear to me. What is amazing to me, however, is that God had in store for me something else…a new life and a new mission, which is in some ways a high mission. I had really never foreseen that "The World" would be "My Parish."

It is a very different perspective to suddenly find yourself standing in your stocking feet, preaching to a hundred people sitting in the living room of a "house church" in the city of Bombay, India. That's a very different kind of preaching for someone who's been used to mounting a wonderful wooden pulpit in a spacious, beautiful, symmetric meetinghouse, and addressing two congregations each Sunday morning of 600 or 700 people each…many of whom are known to you personally and with whom you have deep relationships.

Suddenly, in far-off India, you are not only the stranger, but you are old, white, you do not know their language, and it is hard to see your notes. In fact, a sermon carefully crafted and all written out is neither possible nor appropriate here! The light is bad. There is no amplification. You have to give it to them straight from the *Bible* and straight from the heart. In that strange context…so far from home and from all that you know…you have to speak in such a way, in a language only a few of them understand, that they can see *your* love, and feel

God's love. Despite the language barrier, they can then understand that you have come to them, all this way, from the world Church, as a fellow Christian who cares for them, and tells them the best news they could ever hear.

You have come as a friend, as a brother. Your whole body must say it as stand there, and not just your words in your foreign tongue. You have to, if anything, be more attuned to them and to their needs. You come with news of love for them, for their particular lives, for their church, and for their country.

There, so far from home, in a land with its own religious matters so volatile, your face has to say more, and your being has to communicate more. You can't count on just the words…even though they are the primary medium. Somebody will translate them, but he or she might change some of your words to fit his or her own theological mind-set, as did happen to me in South Korea. What you must try to convey is your heart…and, through yours, the heart of Jesus.

I was brought to the house church in Bombay by a young man who knew English, and who was a lay leader in this church of some thousands of well-educated young business people. This church had previously hosted my young world evangelist friend, David Pierce, who had come to India with his message, his Christian rock band, and his friends.

These folks received me first as David's friend, and also as part of the team…albeit as a father figure among them. There was curiosity and kindness in receiving me. When my preaching was all over, and the people were leaving, it was amazing to realize how much they had actually caught of it, how much they cared, and how welcome I really was.

Even the great crusade, with my dear friend Yesu Bandela and the Gospel Association of India, during which I preached to several thousand largely Hindu people under canopies in the city square of Vijayawada, was an amazing experience. People heard and got it. "Your message in the crusade has made a profound impact on us," a young doctor…member of the Gospel Hall congregation…wrote to me afterward.

With all these people there was a communication of the heart and spirit that was God's work alone, for sure, in reaching people, and in conveying to them these few essential truths about Jesus. Whether preaching at a wedding in Hyderabad, India, to a bride and groom you didn't even know…or standing up in the circle of Masai elders in a village council in northern Tanzania, Africa, or in the little church whose building we helped to build in Kiwawa, among the beloved Pokot…it is often much the same. I have received welcomes so willing as to be almost staggering surprises. People everywhere have been so ready to reach out and receive.

Sometimes, of course, you're more on target in some places than in others. I felt that way in that small church on the hillside in Bukova, Tanzania…the AIDS capital of that country…where I preached in ritual tandem dance with the pastor of the church…in short, almost staccato sentences. The pastor repeated my every gesture, and we competed with the thundering first rain of the season that fairly drowned us out. My teammate, Bill Bieber of Minneapolis, said laughingly, "We've got to do something to get a little more animation and life into you, Arthur!" It was a wonderful experience, even without the benefit of a home congregation, pulpit, or even language.

This has all been a surprise to this old preacher, who has loved to preach for so many years. I loved the crafting and writing of the sermons, the discovery of them, the thinking about them, and the praying about them. I loved doing so here on the front line so far away, in a dark room with no lights, not much by way of notes, and with only one good eye to go on. I loved it in the midst of a setting absolutely alien, yet filled peacefully with the sense of God, of the Holy Spirit at work with power, and of the joy in the room and in my own heart.

Life is so different now. It is so sobering. It is so focused on the Center, the heart, the One, the Reason…Jesus Christ alone. We are focused on holding out hope to people.

Did I *not* do that in all those years before? I think I tried, but now I'm learning to *live* without trappings. I am learning to love and appreciate the "small," to love and be grateful for "alone"…and the journey out across the world alone.

God is teaching me something new and changing me. This is something I need, and may long have needed. I am learning to be glad for what I am learning…and for the freer art of a task that I have always loved so much.

About People

Probably we learn more from pain and problems than we do from ease and plenty. Struggles with people and painful relationships may well have taught me more than the easy relationships. Complex people tend to teach us more too…because they are such a challenge.

In the parish ministry I loved people. I loved being with them, serving them…at their hospital bedsides, at the cemetery as the family gathered in grief, in counseling in my study, over breakfast or coffee in a local restaurant or on my porch. I loved hearing about their lives. I still love the times I'm given with people. I sometimes think I'm really best at just "hanging out"…simply "being there" with people.

I've loved the dynamic of teaching a group of twelve or twenty...or even 70 or 80...when the privilege was mine to hold forth about something I cared about deeply, and when there has been a certain passion to get something you care about across to people. I've loved teaching about the faith, the Spirit, life, and the Gospel of Love.

I have always found people to have something basically good within them. I believe I've tried to look for that and lift it up so the person herself or himself could see it, and be glad for that good thing in his or her life. So, when people destroy, or set out to hurt another...me, or anyone else...there is dismay and disbelief at first.

My last days of parish ministry were hard to understand in that way. Good people...my friends, people with whom I had worked, people I had served...suddenly, behind smiles and public courtesy, worked to diminish me. There was an attempt to convey to others that I was sick, that I was old, and that my preaching was out of touch (with the "modernity" that they had accepted). My preaching confronted them too much about society, morality, values and life style.

When one hears the call of God to tell the truth, and to help God's people find it and walk in it, you know that not everyone will hear it gladly. You know that some will reject it, and that they may reject you. But when that happens...particularly when it is not forthright, when it is not to your face, or when it is indirect and oblique, it is deeply saddening. You may feel betrayed. You surely wonder, *"How could 'my friends' do that?"*

Later, as the years add up and you see these people again, and remember the good times of earlier days, and see how clearly there *was* something real and good of friendship between you, you understand that something happens to human beings, and even to very good people.

They are overtaken. They go through periods of a kind of possession. They are led into doing things that they would never do on their own. A subtle, undercover spirit overtakes their lives. In places like Rwanda, where we have been doing our healing work, people have gone mad with a fear and rage that propelled them to kill. I have concluded, both from the polite society of suburban America, and from the now grieving, guilty, sad souls of the killing fields of Rwanda, that only the demons...whom Jesus so readily recognized, and about whom He so clearly taught us...are the reason for the madness of human life.

This is particularly true when it comes to anger and what we do...even what we do to those we care about the most. Anger, fear, and frustration become madness in our souls and the Devil of rage so easily takes over.

Many socially acceptable plans…if not plots…can lead to this in the desire for power. You tell yourself that you will make things better if you can get your hand on the wheel to get the power for yourself. You will fashion it all so that the inadequate leader is out of the way, the unwanted minister is voted out, or the wife or husband is put in his or her place.

Our thinking is madness. We have been possessed. I conclude that this is true far more often than we imagine.

If we understand this, we will be far wiser in our dealings with people and complex situations. We will be much more fair. We will be far more forgiving.

People are so basically good. The evil they do is often not intended, and when there seems no reason for what they do, there really isn't. They are not themselves. They are taken over by powers from beyond themselves. It has helped me immensely to see…all over the world…how often this is true in the human community.

It is, of course, equally true that every person is God's child. Every person is dearly loved, and *we* must love him or her, as *God* does.

It is central to remember how we ourselves have disappointed God, sinned against Him, and been so greatly forgiven. Suddenly, in seeing the stark truth about human life, we can look at its betrayals, its brutality, its killing cruelty, its enormous injustice…and in seeing our own complicity, actually forgive…as Jesus did. Then we see that "they know not what they do!"

I have learned too, that people all over the world are ready to receive and accept other people who are profoundly different from themselves in color, culture, experience, and age. How we have been welcomed in far countries where we are not even known! People give us a chance. They look into our eyes and feel the language of the heart. That is all the Spirit's work.

About Church

I love "church." I love the process. I love worship, the gathering, the unity, and the power of it. I love the good that church does…in people's lives and in the world's life.

After all these years of working so hard to build a great church, reach out to the community and draw in new members, be on the grow, and do the good thing that growth, money, staff, buildings, and public position make possible, I have learned that "big" isn't the answer. It isn't everything. Even "growing" isn't the only way. Being personally wonderful as a leader…being a great preacher, teacher, pastor, and builder of people and the company called "church," can actually be a trap. These things can be far too important, because in the end it is *people* who count.

Jesus said it over and over, but we still go for "big." This can be wonderful, but when numbers diminish, it is easy to think the world has come to an end. It is easy to make the assumption, "We're failing."

What if you take a hit because of a strong stand you take? What if it is *not* time to fire the leader, but rather the time to pray? What if it is time to regroup and go to the catacombs…"to live to fight another day?"

So much of the ethos of the modern American Church is about growing larger and the importance that comes with growth. Having had it and seen it close up, I realize now it is far less important than so many of us thought it was.

"Church" is the delicate fabric of life woven together by the gossamer thread of the Holy Spirit. What an amazing, fragile network it is! How we need to cherish and protect it.

About Partnership

So much more can be done by taking hands with others, than by thinking you must always do everything yourself. People who know who they are and who others are can have the humility to be partners, working with others in the spirit of a team.

Our Center's partnership with the huge World Vision organization was a remarkable example of what two organizations can do together. World Vision U.S. is a giant fund-raising organization, supporting hundreds of vital humanitarian project in over 90 countries. The work is so important…often responding to crises all over the world. The work of reconciliation was deep in the heart of its former president, Robert Seiple. It was a pain and a passion that he had carried with him since the days when he was a Marine captain flying missions in Vietnam.

Within the World Vision organization, he again and again lifted up the call to reconciliation…in Vietnam, Bosnia, Ireland, and Rwanda, but it didn't quite happen. So many other things were so immediate and pressing.

It was also hard to know how to "do" reconciliation, how to bring people together where so much hurt and awful memories sit between them. A traveling companion to one of World Vision's Africa operations finally said, "Well, if you aren't doing it, why don't you contract with The Pilgrim Center to do it for you?"

This was a preposterous idea! Yet, this great $300,000,000 organization set out to fashion an agreement, a "Memorandum of Understanding," that would make the tiny $200,000 fledgling Pilgrim Center a partner in a five-year commitment to do the work of reconciliation "in the Great Lakes of Africa" (Rwanda and Burundi), and in "the Great Lakes of America" (Minneapolis and St. Paul, Minnesota).

Strangely and wonderfully, after a year of prayer, experimentation, tense travel, intense listening, and laborious work, seven small healing retreats led the way to 25 and then 30 additional healing retreats in Rwanda. These early retreats brought new life to several dozens of Christian leaders in that land. Eventually, grief and healing gatherings were held among a number of Rwandan students at Daystar University in Nairobi, Kenya, and a set of retreats within Burundi also occurred.

It was not all smooth or easy. There were misunderstandings, but the commitment was real. *Partnership* made this possible.

Indeed, the partnership of an older white man from mid-America and a younger black man from Ethiopia working together in committed, faithful, tense work…with a mature white woman thrown into the mix…was likewise a daring attempt at doing a new thing under the rubric of partnership. Indeed, a husband and wife who have shared a marriage of 50 years, and parish ministry leadership of 40 years, suddenly began to travel across the world together, working in strange and tense countries, and offering themselves in the healing and reconciliation cause. This is perhaps an unprecedented partnership that was very quickly recognized by the Africans. "You have come so far, at such risk to yourselves," they said. "We pray for you. You are our family."

It *has* affected our marriage. It is a whole new call upon the life of my wife. She lives with an intensity I was never aware of before. God has clearly called her, and she is determined to go. Energy for her is going out to people half a world away. Time alone together, and energy for that, is in more limited supply. We sit together in our summer office by our lakeside home, and we have faxes, e-mails, and letters for mutual discussion and decision. This cooperation is not always easy, yet it is powered by a Spirit-energy from above…and it is our life. It is so different from the years before.

I am no longer "THE" minister. Molly and I are partners…a team…and things have to be worked out differently. Clearly, it is a *better* way.

About the Gospel's Deepest Message

I thought I knew "The Message"…the essence of the "Good News"…the basics of what God did in Christ for the world. But in the work of reconciliation, in some of the places of most painful difference, and most murderous tragedy in the world, it has become gradually clear that the Gospel's most profound work, the deepest and most central task of the Christian Church as Christ's Body on the earth, is precisely the work of *breaking down what divides people*. It is ending their hate, stilling their desire to kill, and teaching them what Jesus taught 2000 years ago…that is, to *forgive*.

We had to learn for ourselves…these two men who each had painful, betraying, dismaying last days in the organizations we had long served…the hard realities of reconciliation. We had to learn that you cannot afford and do not need to wait for people to say "Sorry" before we forgive them, because some never will. For us to go on, to live life ourselves, and to be instruments of love and His peace, *we* needed to forgive, whether those who hurt us are ever sorry or not.

At this late time in my life, I could be about nothing more important than the work of bringing people home to God, and so home to each other. All the years of parish ministry were clearly specific preparation for this work.

I am beginning to see that this is also Molly's highest call, in addition to my own. It is our greatest challenge. It is our most distinctive and perhaps important work…no matter how much we loved and tried to do well the parish ministry.

About the Most Important, After All

I sit writing on my beloved study dock, on a July afternoon on a clear, crystalline day. The water laps the shore. Sounds come from up and down the shore, of my neighbors at various forms of play. At the dock gently rocks our powerboat that Molly and I have as yet, alas, not mastered.

My dog, Wonalancet, who yesterday climbed the Wildcat Ridge with me, lies at my feet. The sun is hot, the water cool. I have rowed my ultra shell before most of my neighbors were up this morning, and I swam my lengths.

I have a beautiful automobile, the envy of teen-age garage attendants. I live in a simple, lovely cabin among the woods, only a hundred yards from the lake. My wife…my loving, vibrant, selfless, serving friend in the great adventure of life…is here with me.

In Minnesota are a condominium apartment, six grown children, and several grandchildren. If it would be said of anyone, I am "the man who has everything."

I live these summer days in a setting of unmatched natural beauty. My days are quiet…I can do what I love doing: writing, reading, poring over Scripture, praying…alone and with my wife…climbing, sculling, sailing, and swimming.

My hand has pain. Only one eye works and sometimes it dims. But I walk and talk. My mind is whole. I have dear friends who love me and are precious to me in life.

I have a Lord I am privileged to be able to still serve. He grows only more wonderful to me as the years go on. His record of presence, of prayer answered, of unerring guidance given, is perfect. He blesses me daily and calls me. I am on assignment from the King of Kings. I am an Ambassador from the High Court of Heaven...even as I sit here resting, renewing, thinking, and ever preparing.

He is the reason, Jesus my Lord, for my blessing, my abundance, and for all I have. I am of all men most blessed.

But the things, so clearly, are nothing. Jesus alone is everything. If I did not get the grace and honor in my last years as a parish minister...I had more. I had the privilege of suffering for my Lord. If I did not achieve fame as an American preacher, as a "pioneer of the pulpit," I had the privilege of being a shepherd who was good at times to those in the parish years who were given me.

I have perhaps thousands of friends across Africa, India, Korea, and Central America, Australia, the Philippines, and throughout America...friends who know me, encourage me, and are glad for what I've done and been. Many of them are even thrilled at what God has given me to do now.

Being known is a humbling, privileged thing. Most of those in public life have trouble understanding that in the years of our growing, building, or achieving whatever it is we have set out to do. These post parish years, mercifully, have given me time to see the temptations and pitfalls of "big"...whether in churches or corporations. I have seen the tempting pride of leadership and the subtle sin that so easily can overtake all of us "out front."

Somehow, it now becomes a little easier to see and appreciate the eternal things...the living Person of Jesus and His love, the amazing power of His call, and the constancy of His friendship. Within that context is the absolutely amazing gift of a wife who still loves me and in so many ways upholds, stands by, and fulfills me. I also know the joy, pride, and gift of having children...whose lives are a wonder and great honor to me, and the completely unexpected delight of grandchildren whose love is so giving, so joyful, and whose acceptance of me is so complete.

Being in the far country, being amid the longing, need, pain, and grief of Rwanda and Burundi, the fear of Uganda, the hunger of Kenya and Ethiopia, or the volatility of South Africa help me see that the Gospel is everything. They help me know that Jesus stands alone in what is...in the end...important to me.

How glad I am! How eager it makes me for the future.

3

Caring About America: Seeing the World from Africa

It is hard to be an American minister and care about Africa, although it always seemed to me that the Gospel call was to care about and serve the whole world.

The Conservative Christian Congregational group is a small body of the more evangelical among the Congregational churches left over after the 1950's merger of the largest number of Congregational Christian Churches with the Evangelical and Reformed Church, which formed the United Church of Christ. It articulated a concept that the clergy of its churches served Christ *first,* and implied that the world Church was first, and the local church was second.

The local church was to give a minister a ministry. It gave him or her a salary and essentially offered that minister a "base," or a place from which to do "ministry." Of course, that was to be in that local church, and included, of course, Sunday worship, pastoral caring for the people, and regular teaching of "the faith once delivered to the saints." The role of the local church was not to restrain the minister from going out…in their name and Christ's Name…to minister geographically far from them from time to time.

However, the temptation of most parish churches when they "settle" a minister in their midst, is to expect him or her to serve them exclusively, and to keep him or her "only unto them."

If, under God's call, your minister ventures out ecumenically…perhaps even in the company of sister churches and even taking fellow parishioners with him, to a place so far away as Africa, Australia, or South America…it is very easy for some to say: "He's never here. He doesn't really love us. He's not committed to ministry here." This is said in spite of how long you'd served there before you had begun to venture out, and in spite of how hard you may work or how long the hours you keep on behalf of your people.

It is not easy to grow into and keep a world focus to your very local, pastoral, and maybe even deeply personal ministry. The self-centeredness of the whole of American society in the late 20th century is a context that gives added credence to this parochial, narrowly-focused view held by the local church.

It is a curious anomaly that this should happen to a church that has been from the beginning a world institution, with a highly articulated, divinely given world focus. It is even more curious in an America whose business, cultural, and governmental focus has become ever more consciously and seriously world-embracing.

In the latter days of the 20th century, the United States became the super power of the world. Its President was needed worldwide, and he traveled everywhere. American jeans and McDonalds, and the ideas that go with them, are now everywhere. American business is global, as are American homes with their personal computers, e-mail, and the Internet...not to speak of the satellite technology that makes worldwide news instantaneous.

Yet local churches...even large and sophisticated ones...are constantly tempted to narrow their expectations and their faith when it comes to their own family of faith, and how far out into the world they want it to venture. In some cases, these may be the same people who in the rest of their lives are surfing the World Wide Web!

From our mid-American setting, we went to the world because God *called* us to the world. We were not called *away* from the local church...never to come back to those people so dear, who were the daily stuff of our pastoral life. We were called to go out as one goes from home every day to do the work demanded in the world, and then to return, so eagerly and longingly, to ones' own deeply loved people.

God called me to Africa...to the needs of Africa, and the people of Africa...just as clearly as He had called me first to follow Him, and then to be a minister, and then successively to those wonderful congregations He gave me...in little Williamsburg, in changing Newton, and in sophisticated, competitive, successful Edina.

Yet the call was never to go and live somewhere else. It was never to take up the life of a traditional western missionary. It was instead to be the builder of a bridge between the people of mid-America and the heart of Africa.

So I became...more than ever...a journeyer, a "Soldier Pilgrim-Staid," as the hymn says. I was to be a traveler who says to others, "Come along. Let us go out from the places of our comfort, and see what God will show us and teach us, out there where the 'Two-Thirds World' struggles to live."

It has been a venture in taking chances, risking safety, and entering the unknown. It has meant loving unexpectedly and giving freely. It has been a journey of the heart toward personal transformation, toward literally seeing "Life Through a Different Lens."

I believe, because of the journeying out, that I worked harder than I might have otherwise, to "be present" to my people in that wonderfully high potential mid-western city. I loved worship with them. I loved the preaching. I loved the praying. I loved caring as I could for them and teaching others, by example and by specific courses, how to pray, care, and serve their fellow Christians and the world.

It was all a wonder and a joy to me…that strange, wonderful, sinful world of the parish church. It was all that Jesus had…His very Body on the earth.

It may have seemed odd to some former parishioners, if they had ever understood it, but my underlying passion always was for *America*. I loved and I still love this land. While Africa was in many ways the poor of the world, whom Jesus had given me in my call to the ministry, He gave me the poor of America, too. He gave me my sisters and my brothers of all races and backgrounds. He gave me the city. He gave me the great river, the unfolding plains, the high mountains…from "the Whites" to the Alleghenies, to the Rockies, and the coasts "from sea to shining sea."

There has been always for me…

A Passion for America

It is quite simple. God gave America, at the very beginning, to a people of faith. He sent a little company whom we now call the "Pilgrims" across a great and terrifying ocean, to claim a land for Him. It was a unique land, and in so many ways, an untouched land. It was a land in the hands of noble, simple Indian people.

God made the Pilgrims and the Indians friends from the beginning, one people saving the lives of the other. There had been other people to be sure. There was the struggling settlement in Jamestown. There were "voyagers" crossing the great continent from river to lakes and up to Hudson Bay, giving a luster to the wilderness and its northern waterways. With their great canoes they carved out postage paths and water routes, taking their pelts and leaving legends behind.

Jamestown was a commercial settlement. This colony that clung to the edge of the New World at that point within the arm of Cape Cod in that winter of 1620 was a band of brave hearts who came to the great unexplored continent, not for themselves, but for God.

There *was* an economic price. They had to pay back those who had put up the money for their voyage. But they came for the Church, for the Body of Christ. They came to reform the Church they had left behind in England that had persecuted them. That Church had made a marriage of bishops and sheriffs and of Church and State, and it had left no room for venturers of the Spirit. These "adventurers," through the newly-translated Scriptures and prayer, were discovering another way to live the life. The Scriptures had opened up before their eyes a new way of direct access to God through the Spirit.

These young people, these risking radicals, demanded "No King but Christ" as the Head of their church. They had lost patience with their Puritan elder brothers who had thought, by means of patience and time, to slowly "purify" England's Church, and so make it pure and true in the way that the pictures of the New Testament Church brought to life the record of the Acts of the Apostles.

But the young congregation of Scrooby, with John Robinson and William Brewster from Cambridge, and William Brewster from Austerfield, made way with their young friends to Boston…to make a run for it to the North Sea, to Holland and to freedom.

They were turned back in their first attempt and put in the Boston jail…this the very town from which their more conservative Puritan compatriots would themselves not long after come. They would also arrive at the same Massachusetts coast after sixteen years in Holland, departing at last, after false starts, from Plymouth, England.

They came with a burden for Jesus…They came to do a work for Him. They longed, by their example, to change and reform the Church at home, showing that a different way was possible. Their vision was much like the Puritans who soon after began to follow them to the new colony of Massachusetts Bay: "We are as a city set upon a hill, with the eyes of the world upon us!"

They, and the Puritans who followed them, came with a burden for which they were ready to give their lives. Their mission was to "build the beloved community" in the American wilderness, to create a new kind of church. It would be a church led by the Spirit of Christ in its midst, without external human authority…such as that which had become so oppressive in England.

They saw themselves as "God's free people." In that freedom, God would build companies of love, bands of brothers and sisters that would care about and influence the whole of life…the whole of every individual's life, the whole of family life, the whole community's life, and ultimately the life of the commonwealth and the country.

The Mayflower Compact, based on their church covenant of agreement to walk together in love and responsibility to each other, became the basis for their civil life in Plymouth Plantation. 150 years later, America's revolutionary generation took that Compact as the basis for its Declaration of Independence from England, and for the Constitution of the United States.

It was a wonderful and amazing dream of a literal journey out to start new…all over again…to try to get human society right. It was an attempt to get relationships right, to get humility, hope, and nurturing care right. Most of all, it was to try to get right that "this earth is the Lord's, and the fullness thereof," because the land and every human society that is formed upon it is the Lord's. The Lord loves it and will humble it, fill it with hope, and give it a life. According to this vision, the government serves, and the Church cares about the deep things of the human heart and all its relationships.

Their dream was that such a society could be, and that this society could be a light to the world. It could be a light of love, humble service, caring, and sacrifice.

What a dream! What a vision! That was their passion…that America would be this peculiar people, this new Israel, fashioned and found to be a people of service to all people, a people with a care for the whole world. This is also my passion, as preacher, Christian, American, and world citizen to labor still for America yet to pursue that first mission, that "errand into the wilderness" that was the vision that stirred Pilgrim and Puritan alike, as they came to this land on their dangerous journey.

The Insights of Africa

The part Africa has played for me is that the call of God to "come over into Macedonia and help," gave me the world, and it gave one cluster of mid-western churches the world. It gave *world* citizenship to many people in our churches and beyond, who were influenced by the "Africa experience" that became so prominent among us in that first decade and a half.

Suddenly, people who had so *much*, looked into the lives of people who had so much *less*. Here were people not only starving to death…because no rain had come to give grass to their cattle or water to their meager crops of maize…but whose clothes were bracelets and beaded neck pieces, whose skin had pieces of metal grown into it…in the chin and in the ear lobes. The skins of goats were their coverings. Their houses in the little circled manyattas were framed of sticks and plastered with mud and dung. They walked among thorns on a terrain strewn with rocks, and through bushes straining to reach out to catch anyone walking by. "Wait a bit," these thin prickly bushes were called.

What was it like to *live* there and to have that life? What was it like to be there for your entire lifetime, with jagged Mount Kadam in the distance, the sweeping valley floor of the Rift between you, and the brown ridges of the Cherangaries around your shoulders? The Pokot people live dependently on the weather, fearing times of no rain and the resulting desperate scarcity.

Africa, among the famine-ridden Pokot, makes you think about what you have, and what it means...or doesn't mean. America does look different from Africa...or from anywhere in the world. Its opportunity is so obvious. Its wealth is so untouched. It is something very different from what you have, and from what you might have done.

Africa tenderizes your soul. It is hard to return from Africa any other way. You have seen there a certain light in so many faces and a certain kind of freedom...of body movement and instinctive faith...caught by a "We'll see you when we see you" philosophy. This faith is because of Jesus. "If we don't meet here, we'll meet there." The African life of faith is not complicated by the seduction of *things*. After our first trip to Africa, we all came back knowing that we had seen and felt something *different*, the "simple gospel" of Africa.

Seeing Africa's needs, joys, and danger, and yet seeing Africa's hope, forces a reassessment of one's own life and what is important to you. It forces one to examine even how he or she wants or needs to live life. It forces one to understand, as did Stan Mooneyham, the former President of World Vision, that one's "heart is broken by the things that break the heart of God."

So...you change. You are very different. You may be more difficult to live with at home...or so much better to live with. You see with new eyes and you realize afresh the good values. You struggle with what to give up and what to change in your life. Some people become more generous, giving more away. The African people become your *own*, and you want to help.

Africa also helps us understand our differences more deeply as we realize that its hand is upon all of us. We all are sinners, strangers, and sojourners in the world, and Africa makes us more humble in relation to others.

Africa makes you love many places and people. Years ago, the assistant manager of the World Vision project in Antsokia came to my room late at night, and said, "I can see that you love this valley...that it is really yours." And so it was, and is...and when people of Africa say, "Stay. This is your home," you know in your soul that it is so.

The world looks different now and America looks different. It is more unique than ever. It is more loved and missed than ever...even as our hearts have been expanded to embrace the world.

Loving the Least of the Least

Over the years of journeying to Africa, I realized that my call as a minister had always been to the poor, to "the least of the least."

Any ministry I had with the wealthy, the well-off people with such huge capacity, was a ministry on behalf of the poor, and with the poor in mind. It was ministry to the wealthier people there, but also for the poor whom these people could help so much...if they could come to see their own place there and begin themselves, to care.

Serving the poor brings one's Gospel back to center. Jesus' ministry had been to the poor, to "the least." The poor...people with no money or no influence...had all come to Him. They were, again and again, the first to come to Jesus, drawn to Him knowing He loves them all!

That really is what Africa is about, that traveling in a different circle. It isn't nearly as much a racial circle as a spirited circle...among people who are free to love, by His love. In this experience, one begins to see that simplicity in oneself and in others, and he or she understands, forgives, and respects all people more deeply. One sees what needy sinners we are, and it becomes easier to forgive all people...and to believe the best and most hopeful of all people.

In all of this America emerges as a plan of hope for the world. It is a hope that one can help to be fulfilled...in one's own generation.

4

Winning a City Through Media

It is not easy to find a "popular" venue for a viable, honorable, effective mission for Jesus in modern America.

Most of us going into "the ministry" meant the parish church. That was the medium for "doing" ministry. That was the place where the people were, and where the life and work of the Church was. It was the foundation for all other ministries.

While I still believe that to be true, and rejoice in the 40 years God gave me in the Church…as a leader in a rural "country" place, in a struggling, changing, inner-city place, and finally in a growing, powerful, and in many ways "elite" place…I know now that there are other places and venues for ministry.

For example, many of the great para-church ministries have just completed their first pioneering, growing 50 years: World Vision, Campus Crusade for Christ, Young Life, The Navigators, Wycliffe Bible Translators, and more. Others, such as Focus on the Family, have come right along behind.

There are many ways one can be "a minister" today. I, for one, believe more than ever that the local parish church is the basis or heart of it all. That is where the Church of Christ is at its truest. That is where Jesus has promised, through His living Holy Spirit, to *be* "Where two or three gather together in my Name" (Matthew 18:19-20). That's where the people that Jesus said would be the Church, by virtue of His presence among them, would regularly gather. That's where they would meet each other and meet God. They would praise God, sing glory to Him, pray for each other and the world, touch each other with love, and most of all, come expectant "to hear a word from the Lord" through the public reading of Scripture and the passionate proclamation of that Word to them by the preacher.

Church is an amazing dynamic! It is the place where the experience of the Resurrection happens over and over again. Jesus comes, alive in power, week after week, to address His people, to declare love to them, and to offer…in a thousand ways…*life* to them.

It can't be beat, because from that wonderful dynamic, people go out, sent by God, to do the work of ministry everywhere. They go home and love more and do better. They go to the office, be honest, and help others. They go to the city and love the poor, and to the world to serve God's disparate people.

They go teaching as well as preaching. They found schools, seminaries, colleges, and missions. The Church gives birth to it all.

What do you do when you are no longer a parish minister, and you no longer have a pulpit or congregation of your own? What if you no longer have the work that you loved so much, and did so well, and hoped and planned to do for perhaps another five years? What do you do when all that is gone, and you are a "pensioner" according to the Social Security system and the denominational annuity plan?

Do you serve, as you were asked, as an "adjunct" in a local seminary? Do you make speeches or preach sermons here and there, when some other church will hear you? Do you go to the street corners of the world as evangelist?

Many loving people in the last days of my largest parish ministry wanted me to have a ministry beyond the parish. They did not want the ending of the ministry at Colonial to be the ending of ministry for me. Some had a sense, even greater than my own, that my future was to be in mission, that I was meant to be a "journeying-out" kind of guy, and that my calling was really to the world. Some felt it was a far bigger calling than Colonial Church.

"How could it be," I thought, "when I had given my life to that ministry? What could possibly be bigger, or more right for me, than that parish church I loved so much?"

They were right…far more right than I knew. A group of them gathered to help me look at the future. Others worked hard to raise the capital that could make a new ministry possible. A small organization…The Rouner Center for Missions and Ministry…was formed. Some 600 people banded together to create a fund of $100,000 to make a place and a mission possible. Part of that mission would be to continue a ministry in television.

A Face Like This

I suppose it was my own dream, something I had felt deep within, for a long time. Probably from the beginning it had been controversial in Colonial Church: the "Television Ministry"…and that wicked, seductive, and all-powerful medium. The medium of famed "television evangelists," it was so easy to put down and dismiss, and it was difficult to see its point and importance.

We'd had to work so hard at Colonial Church to make it happen, and we'd found funding from largely outside the church. But gradually it gained credibility within. However, it was a ministry to easily view as "ego-driven." This idea is, in fact, the most useful and effective theme that a church body can use against something they don't want to have happen. Then, if you have characterized a television ministry as an "ego-trip," you can also more easily say that the "new church building" and "the journeys to Africa" are also all for the wrong motives. This leads to words such as "he's building a monument to himself" and other themes which supposedly demonstrate "ego-driven" ministries.

Attacking a motive in this way is very effective, particularly in relation to television. After all, television is so much about the *person* on the tube and his or her face becoming known. "This is all wrong," they say. "All wrong."

It's hard to see that this medium, almost and by itself, has become a *teacher* to America…and to my own congregation. It has brought a new culture and values, and it has been so subtle. It has an addictive power, giving "company" in the room to a lonely person. It is insidious and seductive in its power to persuade.

So, why have any part in it…particularly if it is just the minister's ego that wants it? It is horribly expensive. It is an extravagance.

It was very hard for most people to look at the way in which television was also powerful for *good* and the ways it communicates many good things. Some people did believe this and the Television Ministry did happen, in several ways, over a period of almost ten years. The UCC "Project Proclamation" encouraged local pastors of all size churches to try it. They saw the vision of its power to do good and its genius in bringing the audience closer to a speaker than any other means of speech or communication.

Some were just timid, while some were very actively opposed. Others believed that it was a medium that could work far beyond our doors to touch unchurched people with a message that they could not hear otherwise.

I had believed from the early 1980's…with a growing conviction in my soul…that "I could do that." I believed I knew what it takes, and that I had what it takes, and that God would give whatever else it would take.

I had always believed that television could be a vehicle for presenting the Christian message in a different format from that of the usual form and style of the TV preachers. I believed that a different face of Christianity could be shown and that a different spirit could be conveyed. It could be unlike what seemed to be the overdone, exaggerated style of TV preaching. The irenic spirit, which is the heart of true Christianity, could be conveyed through that medium. Perhaps it could be, as Browning describes the young David offering Jesus to King Saul, in his darkness and fear:

> O Saul,
> It shall be a face like this face,
> And a hand like this hand
> That shall open the doors of new life to you!
>   Then
> See the Christ stand!

Somehow, we believed, this medium had the opportunity to show the face of Jesus in a new way to our time.

The Writing of Books

Our new Center also determined to convey Jesus' presence through the *written* word. Though we realized that most books are not for the making of money…and that few authors *do* make money…a book *is* for telling a story. It is for carefully laying out ideas, putting those ideas down in such a way that they may last for a while. If they last for a generation and are read by even a few, they may help make a difference.

So, we are committed to telling the truths that we know…about God, about life, and about the living of life, and therefore I *write*. Our Center *allows* and even encourages me to write. My dear wife Molly also writes…beautifully…about reconciliation. However, she recently pointed out a difference between my writing and hers: "You live to write," she said. "I don't."

She's right! Sitting down to write, with pen in hand…on a legal pad (a very old-fashioned way to do it)…is a way for me to put on paper, and so to discover what I am really thinking. It seems to me that the discipline of putting down on paper the things I know as truth is important to pursue…whatever the result.

We write about Church history, about the ethos and way of Church life, and about ecumenism. We write about love and marriage, prayers, and healing. We write about the coming of the Spirit and His work, about sex and sexuality, and about America and its faith. We write about lives…ours and others'…and about what it's like to do ministry.

It is our belief in *communication* of that wonderful message of Jesus, and particularly of His call to reconciliation, that charges us to use every means possible to tell the world that story. We even put a daily prayer on our telephone "Faith Line" from wherever we are…so that there will be a word of faith for all those who call. These efforts are all part of the "ministry of presence" that God has given us.

The "House by the Side of the Road"

If you mean to have a "presence" in a city, if you mean to conduct a ministry of presence, a ministry of "being there," meeting people where they are, and being a Christian friend to them, then you have to have ways to intercept them. You have to be where they will be, and to have time, and be ready to *listen* to them, to *talk* to them, and be their friend in the midst of the rush of their lives.

As my young "Windpump" brothers say, it is easy for them to be caught in the "Cyclotron of Life"…the busy whirl of activity that catches them up and takes their lives away from them so that they feel as if they are almost serving other gods…the gods of business and busyness, the gods of greed and getting rich, the gods of speed and hurry and getting ahead. If you mean to have a ministry to these folks, you must learn to get into their cycle and circle, and into their hearts and minds, the inner places where they look and long for God.

If I were a parish minister still, I would see many of them after church, in the Common…that sacred place and time for crossing paths, checking in, saying softly how you *really* are, and maybe praying for them then and there…as we gathered together to do in those wonderful days of the parish called Colonial.

But our Center does not do "church." I've jokingly said to some that now "Starbucks is my church!" Just having coffee, quietly talking to someone who chances to stop by…or who has called to ask if we couldn't meet somewhere…I do this now, several times a week.

We also teach in public places early on certain mornings midweek, so people can find and sit with us, and hear of God's love at a local restaurant on their way to work.

Sometimes we gather people secretly and quietly in our homes, just to pray and sing and praise the Lord, and sometimes people simply stop by our Center's office for a visit.

We are busy and our work is never done. But our intention is to keep alive this most important aspect of ministry…i.e., having *time* for people.

During the years of leading a church that was growing larger and larger, it became increasingly harder to find these personal times for people. I often remembered a wistful image from a poet who must have felt like I had in the midst of his own busyness…"Oh, just give me a house by the side of the road, where I can be a friend to man."

5

The One Clear Call of a Lifetime

I always loved the whole of the parish ministry. I loved to preach. I loved to teach. I loved caring about people and, caring *for* them. I loved *being* with people.

The hospitals were familiar places to me. I loved the process of going in, perhaps at night, to the special care unit in the downtown County hospital to see a patient, such as the young man who had jumped…he had hoped to his death…off the 10th Avenue Bridge. His body now lay puffed and broken among tubes and pumps, bandages and respirators. The room was darkened, with only a nurse or two on duty. They were behind the desk at the nurses' station, which provided the major source of light.

I asked to see my young friend, and they accepted me as his minister. Sometimes I was there before some family members, and certainly before friends.

Such pastoral care is "front line." Nurses and doctors do very important things with shots and pills and oxygen and perhaps surgery, but I come with something else…with the love of God and the grace of His healing touch.

There, alone at his bedside, I prayed, with hands laid on that bandaged body. I knew the power of God was there, and that that boy would be touched and healed in his broken spirit as well as his broken body. It was the most important work on earth, and I would drive home through the darkened streets knowing I had been on an errand of mercy under direct orders of the high King of Heaven.

To me, it was all adventure: Going to the weeping home where death was knocking, and there on a bed in the living room, was the wasting one, with one or two family standing by. They would let you in and be glad you'd come. You knew what to say to uphold them, to remind them of what is eternally true, and you would lay a hand of love on the dying one and pray and say what they all wanted so much to say.

You didn't have to stay long. You just had to *come* and they told you that you helped. *You* know that God *always* helps, and His is the help that you bring.

Sunday morning always was high drama for me. It still is, even when preaching in a summer Sunday chapel to only fifteen people. Who are the people who've come? What do they carry in their hearts? What are they looking for?

It's a wonder that they're there…in such seemingly secular days. Yet they come, the thirteen or fourteen hundred…or the three thousand or more on the high days of the great church of your lifetime ministry, or those dozens and scores in the infinitely smaller churches and chapels where you are privileged on occasion to preach.

The expectation, waiting, and listening are the same. What are they waiting for? Are they waiting for a song…great music? Oh yes. Some quiet prayer? For sure. Maybe seeing a friendly face?

More and more, they wait for the experience of being *loved*. Above all, as Karl Barth's mountain people in the Alps on the Sabbath Day, they are waiting to hear "a Word." *A Word from the Lord*. Through some surprising confluence of words, some marrying of idea and language that tells them something from afar, from above, and they know that it is utterly true, and is *meant for them*. It cries out to them. It rings true for them. They ponder it as they leave, and may even speak of it with tears.

How mysteriously it all worked…the experience of public worship! The great organ, the people's singing, the read Scripture, the earnest praying, the announcements of the peoples' business, the church's life, and then the preaching…and the final blessing, as the people touched each other, holding hands as one people, one body, one company of love.

I loved it all. I worked hard to do it all, as well as in the teaching…to show others how to do it and how to pick it up and make it their own.

Perhaps I worked too hard. Perhaps I erred in not sharing more of those privileged pieces of worship and work that were the church's business, and the ministers' business. Surely, toward the end, some complained. "Work smart," one councilman said, "not long." The notion does rise in the modern business climate of downsizing and elimination that more work can be done in fewer hours by fewer people.

Sometimes people offered their helpful advice with the word "*focus*." They said, "You need to concentrate. Don't try to do everything."

I loved to do everything! I loved to do it well. After all, I was on assignment from the King of Heaven! I was an agent of an occupying power. This was critical and important work.

Actually, I also loved to rest! To take the time apart to exercise, to sail and swim, to row and climb, to sit quietly over coffee at table. I loved to be in the midst of my family, to be alone with my wife, or with my children…one at a time or all together in the great holiday gatherings.

But now that that the parish pace is over, I've been privileged to live another life…a life built, I can see now, on the first. I have become aware of something new that God is doing with me. Many aspects of ministry are still here: television, writing, preaching, speaking, being with people in pastoral ways, and "journeys out," which take fellow Christians to far places. But, there is something more…

The Clear Focus on Reconciliation

The work of the Rouner Center was undertaken as it came to us. With September first of 1994, the new life of the past nearly ten years officially began. The old life was often in mind.

But midway through 1996, something happened that was to bring exactly the focus that some friends had wanted to see, and which I quite probably could not have arbitrarily engineered.

We were called, in a new, specific, and defined way, to the work of reconciliation. Out of conversations with a young comrade in Africa the previous winter, World Vision began to envision a partnership with our Center that would allow them to do something they deeply desired to do: the work that is deeper and beyond all crisis feeding, all development of agriculture and water resources, or all orphanage and AIDS work. That work is the bringing of hurt and angry people together in reconciliation.

A "Memorandum of Understanding" was created for The Rouner Center for Missions and Ministry to enter into a five-year partnership with World Vision U.S., to "do the work of" reconciliation in the Great Lakes of Africa (Rwanda and Burundi). It would be a $700,000 project that would last over five years. World Vision would raise part of the funds and our Center would raise part. We would receive a full-time expert from World Vision, our own dear friend, Tekle Selassie, to be our International Program Director, and we would set out to learn and do all we could.

Thus we began. While not frantic, the pace was fast. We knew that we had to earn our way in order to gain credibility within a long-established, giant non-governmental organization and with our own present and future donor community.

Suddenly we were no longer a two-room organization of three people juggling free space in a major office building. Suddenly, there were six of us. We needed space, for which we now would have to pay. We needed to go to the world in a new way, to go where the pain was deepest and find a way to bring people together across their angry, bloody, tribal differences.

We worked! We went three times in 1996 to '97 to Rwanda and Kenya, and finally to Burundi. Our new International Program Director said, "I want Molly on our team," and there we were, traveling together…this mid-sixties white couple and one dear Ethiopian brother.

God did something wonderful with us as a team. He taught us truths deep in the heart about forgiveness and healing. He led us to undertake, and amazingly to succeed in, seven healing retreats in Rwanda that first year. Twenty more immediately followed and we were off and running.

People there were changed, and we were changed. Out of it came the call, the focus for our Center: A call to the work of the human *heart*, the deepest of all work.

I came to see that I had always been about that work, even back at the beginning of the Colonial ministry, and all through the three decades of that life and work. Now mysteriously, it has became clear that this was the heart of what we were to be about. It was clear call and one central focus around which all the other work, all the loved ministry of the past and present could gather and come clear.

It seemed important for us then to change even our name, to call our organization a "Center for Reconciliation." The rest of our work would all be done, but it would find its place around this center…this deep and ever more clear call.

The World Vision Relationship

Going to Africa and doing anything sounds far-fetched and impossible to folks who think you just pack up and go. Over the generations, some have done so, but not our little enterprise.

We have gone with partners to Africa from the very beginning. The first few years we were really guests, and our hosts were a worldwide Christian relief and development agency named World Vision. World Vision has over 3,000 projects in 90 countries. They began their work in Korea, with orphans, in mid-century. Today, 50-some years later, they stand among the most effective, first-response and long-term relief and development organizations in the world.

They were overwhelmed with the early 1980's famine, and came to us in Minnesota saying, "People are dying in the Horn of Africa. Will you consider helping?" Five churches and their ministers responded. We were to be essentially fund-raisers for World Vision's work. That first Easter our five churches raised $369,000, well over the quarter of a million they had urged us to attempt! Eventually, over a dozen years, World Vision estimates we have raised or caused to be raised at least $3,000,000.

We were invited back the second year to go up into Communist Ethiopia. By the second year, I was determined to go on my own, if need be. I went as part of my sabbatical, to be "Pastor in Residence" at Daystar University, Nairobi, for a month. A small team decided to join us for two weeks at the end of that month.

From then on, it became a tradition in the Edina churches to go to Africa. Friendships were being built. Our lives were changing. Our churches were changing. "Africa" was part of our lives.

Visiting our churches in America a year or two later, MacMillan Kiiru, Director of World Vision Kenya, went with some of us to see "Out of Africa." By the end of the film, MacMillan and I, by now dear to each other as friends, were clinging to each other in tears. "For you and me, Arthur," MacMillan said, "it is 'out of Africa' and into eternity!"

Colonial Church decided to build a house in little Kiwawa among the Pokot people, where our teams could stay without displacing any of the missionary community. It still stands high on a ridge above the beautiful valley floor, looking west to little Amadat in the Karamoja country, and on to mighty Mount Kadam, rising jagged and forbidding in Uganda to the west. Later, when the little Kiwawa church was built, I was named as one of its elders. That village and valley, and that mountain and those people, have been in our hearts ever since.

Through the years, Antsokia in Ethiopia was added to our lives, with its experimental farm and water projects. Humbo and Western Abaya followed in the second stage of development after the famine. We had seen the great feeding camps of Alamata and Lalibela, followed by Ibnat and IndeSelassie. We had been to the first in 1983, at Zui Hamersit.

Soon a church was to grow in Mekoy at Antsokia. Colonial became its mother church, and again I was counted among its elders. The "Holy Highway" was built, agriculture developed, and Antsokia became a flourishing center, feeding itself and the nearby city of Desse.

Uganda too, became our home, and First Lady Janet Museveni became our friend. Her UWESO project with children, the Boys' Brigade of the Church of Uganda, and World Vision children and AIDS work all became important projects of our interest, and more and more our passion. Tanzania's Kimokowa and Engekeret, Soweto, South Africa, and Lesotho also became part of our life in Africa, with visits to almost all sites annually.

World Vision was always at our side, often sending a host to accompany us, working out logistics, receiving, and sending us.

Our pattern was picked up and other "Vision Trips" began to happen. God led us deeper and deeper into the heart of Africa…from the stark desperation of starvation and massive feeding camps to the development of water resources and agriculture, to wind pump teams and their three windmills that still pump water in West Pokot, to the dreaded AIDS threat in Uganda and Tanzania, and the Children's Center in Soweto, South Africa, and the women's income-producing projects in the tiny villages of Lesotho's mountain kingdom of the sun.

Finally, World Vision President, Bob Seiple, who had a passion to do the work of reconciliation approached us. This had really been first undertaken in the winter of 1995, as I had been sent with David Montague of Swaziland, into Rwanda. Traveling by Andropov cargo plane, our mission was to prepare the way for a ministry of reconciliation in those months immediately following the April through June genocide, in which a million Tutsi people were murdered, largely by their Hutu neighbors.

After his war experience in Vietnam, Bob Seiple carried a growing conviction that the real work to be done in the world by the Church was the work of confronting the hatred and anger that was causing the wars and the displacement that was in turn creating the large refugee movements, the fear and poverty, and the hunger and killing that was destroying the human community in so many places.

Our Center was charged with raising the first $100,0000 of an initial $400,000 reconciliation project that World Vision wanted to undertake, so we went to see. We visited numbers of people, traveling south and north to find the Children's Center for youngsters whose parents had been killed, or who had fled and simply left them.

We also made the long drive north to the top of Lake Kivu and crossed over into Zaire, spending two days at World Vision's refugee camp, where some 200,000 escaped Hutu refugees were camped. It is that camp that in late 1996 was attacked by Tutsi rebels of Zaire (the early beginnings of Laurent Kabila's army that was to march across Zaire to overthrow President Mobutu.)

We tried to lay plans for a work of reconciliation. I went home to raise the funds, and David set out to design the program.

Our Center did raise that spring about $80,000 before the project went aground in Rwanda itself, apparently over the conflicts that exist continually between relief and development people, and the program/ministry side of World Vision's work. However, before it ended, our Center had paid for the beginnings of a very important weekly radio program in Rwanda that offered a reconciliation theme.

Twenty thousand of the dollars raised were allocated to Burundi, and I went into that country in the winter of 1996 to meet with Philippe Guiton, then

World Vision Burundi Director. The mission was to meet people, see some of the work being done in reconciliation, and make together some determination of what those monies could support.

So early on in the life of the Rouner Center, the call to reconciliation had come. Already we had visited places that later were to be on the front pages of the news. Later, in our "formal" partnership with World Vision, a new day came.

In the first year we ventured into Rwanda, World Vision encouraged ties with other organizations. Between our second and third journeys of 1996 to 1997, we undertook healing retreats for pastors under the aegis of the Evangelical Alliance of Rwanda, and later with the staff of the Protestant Council of Rwanda, Youth for Christ, and the female leaders of the Evangelical Alliance…from all of the prefectures of the country.

It was an intense, wonderful year…a year in my life built upon sure and lasting foundations which had been lain by the people of World Vision. They became our friends for life and our understanding, helpful partners.

The Great Lakes of Africa and America

The official charge of our partnership for the five-year undertaking in reconciliation was to go to the "Great Lakes of Africa and the Great Lakes of America." These translated into the two small Tutsi and Hutu dominated countries of Rwanda and Burundi, and the Twin Cities of Minneapolis and St. Paul, Minnesota, where World Vision is directly present as Vision Twin Cities.

We initially discovered that we were viewed as "newcomers" to the field of reconciliation. Even though we had been substantial donors and raisers of funds, suddenly…even though with the agreement and invitation of World Vision itself…we were perceived as "invaders." Some of the hard-found money that would be spent on this venture was money that other projects in World Vision would love to have had to apply to some of their already-established programs.

In journeying to Africa with the Windpump Team, even some of our friends and partners in other projects took a somewhat diffident stand: They were not yet ready to embrace us as co-workers in the enterprise of healing the hurt heart of Africa.

It was a little bit of "Jesus I know, and Paul I know, but who are *you*?" Were we old Africa hands? Were we trained in the standard processes of World Vision? No!

"You didn't consult with the field in setting up the project," one of our friends said. "I never heard about it until it was an accomplished fact."

We wondered why our visionary partners back home at headquarters had not communicated with the field. We assumed they had, so our arrival in Rwanda was somewhat of a surprise. Headquarters had assured us that we did not need to work *through* World Vision Rwanda. We could make our own contacts, which we did…first with the Evangelical Alliance, and then with Youth for Christ.

The retreats undertaken there, especially the first, were held in God's blessing and brought results far beyond our expectations. "I am not afraid anymore," one pastor said. Another told us the moving story of his forgiving and taking into his own home in his family village, a man, once landlord of the house he was occupying, who had murdered the whole extended family of his friend.

We learned so much that year, of how reconciliation really *is*…especially that you not wait, if wronged, for those who wronged you to come and say, "I'm sorry." We also learned that God had done the work of preparing the way for us. We are His, and He treated us with honor and respect, and He had "sent His holy angel before us to take us safely to the land He has prepared for us."

Tilting at Windmills

We readily admit that we must have looked at the very beginning much like Cervantes' Don Quixote, riding out ridiculously, tilting at windmills, thinking we were doing something serious, engaging the dark dragons of the land, defeating evil and hatred, and bringing love back to its rightful place.

Could we not see the real dragons of our time? Did we not understand the horror of what had happened in there countries? Did we not understand the danger…to ourselves, as well as those people there we were trying to help? We came on our ridiculous mounts, put on our tinny armor, and dashed off to take on the deepest human problem of a whole nation.

On such an errand, you *have* to believe that you are in God's hands and that He, after all, is the Chief Justice here. *He* is working *His* agenda. We are in *His* plan. So, we pushed on.

Suddenly, at the end of the first year, the people in World Vision and in the funding world had the chance to look at what we had actually done in the first year of our scramble to be credible. They saw the fruits of our work to establish a beachhead of brotherhood among the people so desperately needing to find each other and be healed.

The news started to come back; "Hurt people have been set free. Deeply wounded people have been healed. A new dimension and network has been forged. Beyond 'How-to' seminars, here is something that frees people to do the work the seminars told them to do, but which never healed them to do. There have been breakthroughs here."

Those who before had only tentatively held out on us, now began to uphold us...making sure that this new thing had a chance to happen, live, and grow.

Finding a Way to Begin

It was the genius of our colleague, our Ethiopian brother, our "International Program Director," that sensed instinctively that we were not called to offer another seminar. He knew that we, as friends in Christ, were not called to come and tell people *what to do* to bring about healing in their land. We were to go in the simplest way, offering ourselves, but far more, offering Christ. If we could lead people to the foot of the cross, something would happen to them there that would be from God, and that they *would be healed*.

We were after all, the Church coming from across the world to be with them, to stand beside them, to bring the love and caring of the world Church, offering it and seeing what God would do.

As a team we were, after all, a 40-year parish minister with experience in the healing of the human heart...We were an Ethiopian...an African...with fifteen years of experience as a World Vision Country Director in three different African countries...And, we were a mature and wise woman, mother of six grown children, grandmother to four, a former administrator in an international health organization in Minnesota, and a behind-the-scenes leader in three Christian churches. Two of us were white and one was black. Two of us were old...in our middle to late 60's...and the other nearly two decades younger.

We were not simply an "odd couple" or a triumvirate of has-beens. We represented years of experience in the life and way of faith. We knew something about brokenness and hurt. We had been around.

It was natural to us, as well as a clear leading of the Spirit, that we came to sit in a circle with the brothers and sisters God gave us. We were not above them, and we were not experts. There was only the Holy Spirit's agenda. We offered them a "place" to open their lives and receive the healing of Jesus.

At first they introduced themselves. We sang and prayed. The second day we invited them to bring any hurt to the table...for on the table was a simple wooden cross...and allow us to gather around as a group and pray for them.

For twelve people, this took all day. The table flowed with the tears of these supposedly emotionally unexpressive Rwanda men.

The last day we bent before them, and washed their feet as a sign of Jesus' call to servant ministry, and then shared with them the Lord's Supper. It was utterly simple, completely Biblical, essentially pastoral…something each pastor among them could do with his own people. It was a little model. There was no agenda but the Spirit's, and no notebooks but the participants' own experiences and memories.

What was remarkable was what God did, through His amazing and powerful Spirit, as He moved in among us, as this company gathered together. He did deep within them what they said no numbers of seminars, no pages of instructions, no agendas had done. We were amazed…at the little place God gave us to begin.

All of the Church's Experience Feeds This

Boris Pasternak once said, "Nothing goes ever traceless, lost." Each experience of life has its place, its purpose, within the "plan." My own experiences as parish minister…the high times and the painful, dark times…have all fed into this attempt to be available as an agent of reconciliation. The study of the Bible, the words of preaching and teaching, the learning to listen, and the willingness to care, have all been useful…even though this work seems to be such virgin territory.

After all, the work of the ministry is work…supremely…with *people*. It is work with the human heart. It is work with the broken spirit. It is work with the healing God, Who Himself made the fact abundantly clear.

Molly and I had loved the work. We both knew how to do it. We both cared. Tekle too, had spent his life in the midst of people's needs. We were there literally to be *used*. We wrote notes, we made outlines, but mostly we listened to God and spoke as He prompted us.

The painful experiences of diminishment and rejection that Molly and I had experienced…from people very close to as in the church so long, and, we believe, so well-served in the life of the church…God used for *good* in this new work, this terribly important work that He had prepared for us. Tekle too, had experienced rejection from the great Christian organization he himself had served. So he too, came to the work of reconciliation out of pain.

We all knew something of the killer instinct of those who hate you. We knew something of having to see people regularly in social places, who…if the truth be known…we didn't much want to see. But Jesus taught us to forgive them. He taught us to love them. This is the lesson we learned from the very people we came to help in Rwanda.

The Call to My Wife

Perhaps the most dramatic change that came in the first of these "post-parish" years, in the first year of the Reconciliation Ministry assigned under the partnership with World Vision, is what has happened to my wife.

Our International Program Director came to us in September, having made it clear as the "Memorandum of Understanding" was being fashioned in midsummer, that he wanted Molly to be part of our Reconciliation Team.

I suppose I did not know what that meant. I am not sure Molly knew what that meant. But it soon became clear that her head and heart were needed to keep us straight, to help us deal carefully on spending, written understandings, and accounting for all that we did. Molly has a mind…to grasp concepts, to articulate truths, to write and tell a story directly, almost tersely, without frills.

Tekle saw her place before either she or I did. She was clearly to be part of the "traveling team." She would journey out with both of us, and do some work that I could not do. She was not merely accompanying me.

She was eager to go. She never flinched or demurred. She never said, "Look here, I'm a grandmother, my family needs me, and I'm staying home!"

In fact, a series of journeys took me away in October…one to Korea, and another to Nashville, Tennessee, with my brothers and sisters of Churches Uniting in Global Mission. When I returned from the latter, Molly and Tekle had already left for Nairobi and the preparation work we were to do there for a series of peace courses at Daystar University.

When I arrived in Nairobi in early November, Molly had already been there for three days. We had meetings there, then journeyed together…the three of us…to Kigali, Rwanda, where we met pastors in Byumba in the north and others in Kigali. We visited government leaders and church leaders, preparing the way for the retreats we'd do in March, and perhaps again in May.

When March came, I had already flown in from India. Molly and I journeyed to western Kenya to be at the little seminary where I had taught ten days in the previous year. With dear friends we drove first to Mount Elgon to visit ministries there, and then ventured north to our beloved Kiwawa, where two wonderful, miraculous days of reconciliation within the young divided church was waiting for us.

Later, while Tekle and I traveled to Kiwawa, Ethiopia, Uganda, and Tanzania with the Windpump group from home, Molly was bringing Rwandan students from Daystar University together, for several weeks of their own healing.

Then it was on to Rwanda and a pastors' retreat. Tekle had already done one retreat, but we joined him in this one, which turned out to be the high point of our year! For three days, we sat with these young men, some Tutsi and some Hutu. All were pastors, some with very great struggles since they had come back to Rwanda. The circle formed, with the cross our center.

They were deep days. We saw the very brokenness of their souls come out. We heard their stories…from the genocide, the war, and even from their own parish lives. It was a walk through a dark valley. We needed prayer, the whole armor of it. We needed that armor much more than we realized when, upon our return, Molly was asked to tell the story of Rwanda to her friends in the women's church circle.

It was too much. Our own vulnerability was too great. The medical tests and the incident of temporary memory loss taught us how always critical is our need for protective armor. The danger to us would not be small airplanes…or hard driving over mined roads. The danger was the work itself…and its setting. We were in the killing fields of Rwanda. A million people had been killed there in three months, most of them by their neighbors.

The Devil had held sway. He had possessed these people. Why would He relinquish His grip on the throats of these people when He had so successfully wounded this land? Who would He fear most, if not those who came to help this land's healing in the Name of Jesus? Of course, He was there to prevent the possibility of healing and hope for the future.

Molly's temporary memory loss was a worry to our children, of course. But she had come back free of physical complication. To our grown children who feared losing their mother, my answer came to be…by God's gift…"You must understand. This is the first great call of God upon her life…to her own deep and highly skilled ministry. She accepted her call to raise her children and to be at my side in ministry all these years. She is doing now what God has called her to do and prepared her to be."

That first year was intense. Molly has been directed as never before. Her stature has grown and her spirit deepened. It is a very new day for her, in faith, as it is for me.

6

Who Are We Among So Many?

Rwanda and Burundi are very small countries. Rwanda's border in any direction can be reached by car from the capital city of Kigali in about two hours. Rwanda's entire population is about eight million, but in three months' time…from early April through June of 1994…800,000 to a million people were murdered, most of them by their neighbors.

It is a prospect so frightening as to be almost incomprehensible to most of us in America…despite our "mean streets," our glib and largely unthinking acceptance of abortion and what it is doing to many human lives each year, and so much that is angry, violent, and predatory in American social and family life.

When we think of the sheer scale of a million people being cut down…largely by machetes…in such a short time, we realize that just a few people can't do that…maybe not even 50 or 500 people.

During those terrible days, there were killers everywhere…ordinary people, filled with fear, who acted on the commanding instruction of their government issued over the radio. "The Tutsi's are coming," the message said, repeated over and over, referring to the rebel army moving inexorably down and across the country from the north. "They will kill you, unless you kill them first. You must kill your Tutsi neighbors, your Tutsi in-laws, your Tutsi colleagues at work."

It appears that this madness was not even questioned. The country was at war. Fear held sway there, in every heart. People did what they likely would never have done otherwise. That is probably the only explanation, because nothing about the genocide can be logically or reasonably understood. A strange madness took over a country, a madness accompanied by a sense of fear greater than a spirit of revenge.

The signal for it to begin was the downing of the Rwandan president's plane just as it returned from a peace conference in Tanzania. The plane actually crashed in the president's own backyard. With that news, the killing spree began. Many believe that it was all prearranged, and that the genocide itself had been carefully planned two years before. For such horror to be premeditated seems unthinkable.

But it happened. Some of the rivers of Rwanda were choked with the murdered bodies that had been thrown into it, as village after village was systematically murdered. Bodies were piled up along the roadsides, even in the capital city. Dogs began to feed off the dead bodies, their taste for human blood then turning them to attack living human beings. The dogs had to be killed to prevent their cutting down of humans.

As people were murdered and their houses torn apart, pieces were carried away. It was altogether a strange, hellish nightmare. As the rebels came ever closer, the killers, largely Hutu, began to flee. Some of them were militia, who had been trained in the streets by the French, but many of them were next-door neighbors, who picked up machetes and butchered those around them whom they feared.

Then the army of rebel Tutsi's came...back from the countries where they and their ancestors had previously fled...and suddenly, they were the new government. They toppled what Hutus were left, and they...so young...became the new government.

The bodies are gone now. The dogs are gone. Families are desolated. Grief lives everywhere, as do anger and a terrible sense of injustice.

The new government seeks to do justice. They have set up tribunals. Hundreds and hundreds are in prison. They beckon all to come home from the refugee camps. "If you are innocent, you have nothing to fear," the government says. But what if they are not innocent?

Many refugees have come back, and have gone straight to their own villages, where suddenly they have been face-to-face with the very people whose families they had murdered. They look each other in the face. "Welcome home," they may say. "I recognize you...You are the one who killed my so-and-so." What a dynamic...and they must find a way to live together.

Some of the returnees have tried to eliminate those who know what they did, and who would tell, but the young government seeks to do justice if it can. Its invitation to those in the refugee camps has always been, "Come home. Be a part of the rebuilding of our nation. If you are innocent, you will be safe. If you are guilty, you will be tried in the tribunal, but we will be fair. Dare to come home."

Here was this little country, governed now by men...many who had previously even left the country. Rwanda had seen Tutsi tribal people leave the country in several waves in the past...some having gone to Zaire, some to Uganda, and some to Tanzania.

Many in the rebel army had left years before. But now they had returned, and had taken up the reins of government. Others, Tutsis who had also left over the years, returned from all directions and began to replace the near million who had been murdered in the 1994 genocide.

All types of new people now lead the grieving, wounded country. Many present pastors have themselves come back from lives away. Often they have founded new churches with new names, because they do not want to be identified with the churches that failed in the dark time, those that were compliant with the Hutu government that would finger them for murder.

The reality is that this land can only live by its people finding a way to live together. Only a real measure for forgiveness will make that possible.

Can the knowledge that others have murdered ever allow people to live with them and accept them? It is humanly impossible, and the country will be finished if it doesn't happen.

Curiously, the Rwandan government believes that the Church is crucial for this recovery. Only be regaining its credibility in the eyes of the people of the villages will its necessary leadership in the most difficult arena of forgiveness become possible. The Church must find itself, the government says. The question then, is…

Where to Begin?

Where does the country begin? And where does the world outside that wants to help, begin?

Some of our closest friends wondered how our small Center could possibly do anything that would be effective toward reconciliation in a country so far away, among people with such terrible memories and deep hurt, where people's heritage and history is so different from ours. Some, at the beginning, were not even willing to financially support that part of our work.

Besides assisting returning refugees in food and medical assistance, the outside world…even the world of the Church…has tended to concentrate on teaching leaders, especially pastors, how to understand and heal the trauma that grips their country and their churches. Seminars are being given in large numbers. Notebooks are handed out, and lists and outlines are put up on the blackboard. Experts sit up front…often higher up. They hold forth, and explain all in human psychology for dealing with trauma aspects.

For us, there was so much we did *not* know. Rwanda's history was itself so overwhelming. However, the connections began to grow…especially after our first assessment trip in November of 1996…and we began to learn what the pastors and people wanted and needed, which was someone to *listen to them*, and to *talk to them*, from the world's perspective.

The fifteen pastors, who had allowed us into their peace-building committee meeting that cold day in mid-November 1996, listened first to us. And somehow, we were led to say the simplest things we knew. "We are here from far away, because the world cares about you, the world Church cares about you. We come in His name, and we know, as the Church across the world knows, that only one thing heals: repentance, confession, and forgiveness."

Tekle talked to them about repentance, preached to them, and then wept as he spoke. "You must repent," he said. "You must confess all, and God will heal. That is His promise. That is *our* promise. We are here to stand with you."

We were in Byumba, the first section to be devoured by the war that had led to the genocide, and their people were devastated. They were Hutus, and now they were desperately poor. At first, I'm sure they hoped to receive money from us. One pastor said his people were so poor that they couldn't get on with the work of reconciliation. I said, "You know, I served a church so large and wealthy that I too, could not get to the work of reconciliation." Suddenly everything broke open and they were begging us to stay. They would have us, as long as we had come truly, to be "present" with them.

By the time we had met with four more pastors in Kigali, it was clear that our call was to very simply offer the Gospel, the host of Christ, and the blood of Christ for their healing. The conviction grew that we must offer the most basic thing...the Biblical, spiritual, faith-based thing. We knew that we were to start with the Church, we were to start with its leaders, and we would be working with the leaders' healing first.

We would not attempt seminars, lectures, or "How-To" lessons on anything. We would come from our Christian base, from our Church understanding, from the *Bible* that we believe, and from the prayer that so satisfies us. We would trust the Spirit of Christ to reach out through the cross and the blood...to healing and forgiveness and freedom.

The Problem of the Rwandan Church

Rwanda is a Christian country. At least the great majority of its people were nominally Christian, approximately 65% Roman Catholic and perhaps another 25% Protestant.

However, in the month of April 1994, when the word went out from the government to make their country a killing field, the Church did not rise up in protest; the Church did not officially say no.

The Church, in fact, had enjoyed enough favor with the Hutu government, that when the choice came between the Church's many relationships and informal ties with the government…or the loss of them all by confronting the government…the Church for the most part remained silent. Those few individuals who did speak up were killed, so the Church in many instances hung its head and said nothing. In some cases the Church was even compliant by allowing murderers to come to a church building and kill the people who had sought sanctuary there.

So the Church had failed in leadership in the very moment that it was needed most, and people *knew*. The stature of the Church fell to desperate lows as confusion covered the country and its people fled. There were a few heroes…such as Antoine Rutayisere…who later led the movement for reconciliation, but in the eyes of many Rwandans, the Church had been compromised.

Yet the Rwandan Church is still needed. The faith of its people needs the Church's teaching and encouragement. Since the possibility of healing lies in forgiveness, this is the Church's business. Now the government still asks for the Church to work to regain its credibility and to take up leadership again.

It was in standing with a restored Church that we felt we could make a difference. Our opportunity would be to help the Church. This help was so deeply needed because the Church had fallen so far. It needed to recover not only the place it had, but also to claim a new, more humble role of leadership. The Church itself had to become a chastened, forgiven place of confessional power in order to lead a confused people into a new faith that has the courage to stand steadfastly before the cross.

Beginning with Pastors and Organizations

We began, actually, where we were invited to begin. As we look back and see it now, we see that this was God's direction.

When we first went to Rwanda as a team just to meet people, to make friends, and to establish contacts for later work, a young man from Ghana named Godfrey eagerly welcomed by. He had written to us, urging us to come. He was World Vision Rwanda's "Reconciliation" officer.

One day Godfrey drove us north from Kigali to Byumba to sit in on a meeting of the country's Peace Committee. Godfrey had been meeting with this group, and in fact, he was probably the one who had actually gathered them together. He had done major work to persuade the pastors of these widely different traditions to come together, including the writing of a lengthy proposal paper…essentially to World Vision Rwanda…which urged the development of a total Reconciliation Ministry.

At least one Catholic priest was at the meeting. Each of the others represented a different denomination. It was Hutu country and their work was hard. They begged for support.

The story of that meeting has already been told, but the point is that fifteen men…all pastors…had gathered together to talk about ways to find peace. They were going to work that day on plans for the organizational constitution. This project that was soon was left behind as we become engaged in the *real* questions of peace.

After that unusual, openhearted visit, we drove back to Kigali, and the next day we met with several more young ministers whom again, Godfrey had contacted and brought together. Unfortunately, it was at about this time that quietly and carefully, Godfrey informed us that he was being transferred from his position, if not actually being let go. We could see no reason, since all we knew was of his passion and absolute commitment to the work of reconciliation. We wondered if it could be that "reconciliation" itself was just too much of a challenge, and that Godfrey's piety and enthusiastic evangelicalism was just too much for the "relief and development"-oriented people of World Vision Rwanda.

In any case, another, much smaller group of pastors gathered to meet with us in the World Vision office. That second meeting started off as cordial and polite, but soon became animated and eager. One young man in the group…thin and spare, angular and alive…held forth at length about his recent visit to the refugee camps and his belief that a real ministry could be undertaken there. He was excited about the possibilities, but even more he was excited about *renewal*, about people catching the spirit of the of the hour, the *kairos* for evangelism that he believed lay at the heart of any renewal that was going to come.

His arms flung wide. His movements were expansive. His whole face seemed lighted up. He was Jean Pierre Kamanzi. The next day as we showed up at the Kigali Airport, Kamanzi and his boss from the Evangelical Alliance were there to see us off.

So that is where we really began. By March, Kamanzi had gathered twelve pastors out of the Evangelical Alliance to share a retreat of three days with us. So we started with the Church that so needed redemption, and with partners who knew *they* must be healed if ever their people were to follow.

Each of these pastors had a flock. Any change, or any light ignited in them, would have a chance to catch fire among their people. It was a beginning, and one that four months later God honored.

The people who usually clambered on Russian cargo planes in Nairobi, to take the chancy ride across the lake to drop down in Kigali in the winter of 1994 to 1995, were invariably young, seemingly single, and of almost a hippie variety...long-haired, fast-talking, confident-appearing people in wire-rimmed glasses, old jeans, loose shirts, and small packs. They went under the banner names of Care, Feed the Hungry, the United Nations, and even WORLD VISION.

They were thrilled to be there, and it was high adventure for them. Many had been trained in the finest schools to think globally and governmentally, and they did not seem to be particularly "pious." They were good-hearted, and they certainly had a sense that they were *doing good*. These urbane, highly trained young people often represented the United States in its own agencies abroad. They were typical.

They were far from being tourists, and they are certainly were not military or Secret Service. They were young good hearts, God bless 'em. They had taken chances, run risks, and been America's best foot forward in meeting human needs around the world...serving refugees in the camps, and believing in the poor.

Back home they would likely be the young political liberals who are highly ideological, and who care about "the right thing." However, they were often not sure of what is the *foundation*, the "Rock of Ages" that underlies "the right thing."

Even World Vision, the vast, wonderful, world-wide helping organization, clearly motivated by the call of Christ, and seeking to work out and live out His ethic in the life of service, tends to have its "cowboys" who love the thrill of the crisis, and who know just what to do to meet its exigencies...whether of starvation, water and land reclamation, orphans in the streets, or organizing great camps of refugees.

But then, along came the small team who had all their lives done something quite different: a 68-year-old minister "beyond the pulpit," his wife of over four decades, and a 50-year-old mighty believer from Ethiopia...all of them full of faith, and if anything, "pious" in their mode and purpose. How naive and obvious they must have appeared when compared with any of those around them!

Their resources seemed scant, and even some of the best supporters in their enterprise...by later admission...were skeptical and uncertain about their venture into reconciliation. Even some deep in World Vision's hierarchy itself viewed this little group as nearly non-players or strictly marginal on the edge of an enterprise in which World Vision's President had already invested so much. World Vision's fundraisers had already had been having such a struggle in helping the donor world to see understand and get behind this seemingly quixotic enterprise.

But, we felt God's hand. We saw infinite possibilities, and we knew that in these first two years we would have to go for broke, working hard and tirelessly. We would have to take chances personally if we were to evolve any sort of model of reconciliation and gain any degree of credibility to allow us to then build, grow, and do the good we knew we had been given to do.

Unlikely we were, in the world's terms…and perhaps even in the Church's terms. But our mighty Ethiopian man of faith had seen instinctively what a wise woman of age and maturity could mean in this healing ministry. He saw what a pastor's years of experience would bring, and the advantage there was for an "old man" within an African culture that loves and respects old men. And he saw what a rare partnership it really was, in America or anywhere, for white and black to work together in a ministry that needed to show and live the reconciled life that we would be trying to offer God's wounded people.

Looking back, it seems very clear that is was God who knew what He was doing, and who was laying plans ever so carefully as He gathered by faith, those who would lift high the cross of Christ in the cause of reconciliation.

7

Healing the Grief of Rwanda

As I sat on a blue afternoon in North Hampshire by the lake I love, Rwanda seemed so far away...and its grief so awful and unassuaged...that the notion of being part of any healing of the whole land's grief seemed preposterous.

Could I do that? Was I about that? Could anyone do that...go to others in their pain, and help them heal?

And then I remembered Jesus...for that is exactly what He did, and what He calls us to do. As for me, I was not sure that I could bear it, without myself "coming apart and resting awhile."

It wasn't the missionary pattern. It was nothing the great missionary organizations would set up. But for the unusual team that God had brought together, I believed that it was right, and that God was making it work.

He has given us a life with both ebb and flow. He has provided a certain balance: a summer time to think, rest, reflect, wait, plan and prepare. That is followed with weeks of intensity...of traveling back out to those so distant places, and going to the depths with people...and listening, listening, listening, and praying. We are with them. We are present.

It is a strange turn of life for me, so different from the busy round of work that a large parish entails, where one must change moods and modes a hundred times a day, and spend so much time on fashioning a frail organization and attending fragile egos. These are of course important...but are they the first line of the Gospel?

It is no wonder to me that Paul wanted to be on the road, to be "out there" across the world. He was doing the most essential thing: delivering the message and telling the wonderful truth.

In these days of "post-parish" life, nothing seems deeper to me than dealing with the hurts of the human heart. It is so important to be present at the places where hearts are broken, and where needs, spirits, families, neighborhoods, cities, and countries, are broken.

With each passing day of prayer and thought, of reflection and understanding, it all comes clear that *this is the work*. This is the call. This is the life...for now: healing the grief of Rwanda.

We do a small thing. We do not lecture. We do not preach. We do not give what Africa knows as seminars. We do not tell those people what to do. We go simply to *be* with them, and to let Jesus come and do the healing that is needed in their hearts.

How do you do that? You ASK Him. You INVITE Him.

The Retreats

For our first retreat there were many competing events. One or two of the pastors were going back and forth between a large reconciliation seminar and our retreat.

The participants expected formality. They expected to be *told*. They expected a blackboard, a syllabus, individual shiny notebooks, and a clear agenda.

We sought to disarm them at the beginning. "We are prepared," our International Director said, "but we are waiting for the agenda of the Spirit to emerge. He knows what we need to do together for these three days. We come to meet before the cross as brothers and sisters. There are no experts here. Jesus is here, and we look to Him. He will help us find the healing and help we seek."

That whole first day, we talked about our lives, essentially introducing ourselves and especially talking about the cross. We laid out a theology of the cross, and the power of the blood of Jesus, sacrificed for us, to work change in our hearts...cleansing us, forgiving us, and healing us. We prayed and sang, almost instinctively and spontaneously it seemed.

The second day began with singing and a devotional time, led by Molly. At one point, to my surprise, she introduced the issue of pain in our lives, and asked me to help them begin.

I had prepared other things, if needed. But it seemed right then to say, "I have had some painful things. I too, like you, am a pastor. I gave my life to my people for 32 years, but in the end an angry murmur began and there was betrayal and deep hurt for me, as people misunderstood my ministry and sought to undermine it. I have had to live with grief about all that...and the pain of remembering."

Perhaps they did not know that these things ever happen to an older pastor...or a white man for all of that, but my words apparently encouraged them to open up the secret hurts in their own lives...especially in their lives as pastors.

So they began...each telling of some pain in his life...of what had happened to him personally in the genocide. They talked about what had happened to hurt them in their pastoral lives.

Seven and a half hours later we were done. Each participant had spoken at length. Each one had been prayed for with the laying-on of hands, kneeling at the little table that held the cross. They knelt to pray, to weep, and to cry out. The others gathered around and held them, touching and praying for them. They sang. The table was awash with their tears.

Our team went home to rest, talk, and prepare. The pastors, however, gathered then for more prayer at the table in the evening! By morning they were greeting us with hugs and smiles…these supposedly undemonstrative, unemotional Rwandan men!

We gathered again in our little retreat room. Tekle introduced the day. They were ready with water and towels, and we began with foot washing and a teaching from John 13 on "Servant Ministry." After that we shared communion.

Again there were tears. We knew that we were participating in the historical rites of the Church. They all understood, and it took all of us to the depths.

We talked for a while of evaluation…of organization…after this beginning. At the very least, a follow-up was begun. The pastors resolved to continue to meet and to uphold each other.

We had begun.

The Friends and the Longing

The grief of Rwanda is of course, profoundly complicated, and we remain…if not amateur…then certainly humble learners.

Each of the first seven retreats that we conducted in 1996 to 1997 was slightly different from each other. We slowly began working at creating a basic model of approach that would lift up and touch the wounded or broken heart. It would begin at the point of inner healing, of setting free the inner heart, and of opening the way for forgiveness to take place in all lives and organizations.

The leaders who began working with us…Youth for Christ, the Protestant Council of Rwanda, the staff of two local churches, the original twelve pastors, and a group of representative women from across Rwanda…began to see that what they were doing had embraced several questionable notions. For example, they had assumed that a "seminar" would change people, and that to simply be *told* what to do equips one to do it.

Our healing retreats, so unlike seminars, opened the way for actual individual and group experiences of *healing*. The people present saw how the healing had happened, and how the process had worked. Here was a new dynamic that seemed to those leaders to have a greater chance for success, so proposals began coming for an entire series of retreats…reaching widely across Rwanda…from the groups that experienced the initial taste for what God can do in such a setting.

Deeply in our favor has been the longing throughout Rwanda. We are not dealing with simply a good idea. We are dealing with something that carries authentication within it as it plays itself out. It is in itself a demonstration of what can happen. This process is so pastoral, so Biblical, that the participants themselves are able to pick it up and make it happen again later by their own leadership.

The longing is everywhere in Rwanda for healing. Many organizations are finding it difficult to do their own work because of the trauma felt by their own staff. Pastors and other individuals know that they are themselves, literally, "stricken" with grief, and that something needs to open up in them. That is perhaps why news spread so quickly across Kigali and its Christian community and agencies about the dramatic results that came about at the Pilgrim Center retreat.

Here was something that worked. Here was something that seemed to be an answer. Unburdening, healing, freeing, and a newfound holy form of forgiveness was just what people longed to hear about.

Our work also involved many personal relationships. We met the wife of the leader of the Presbyterian Church in Rwanda, and went to see the work she was doing with a group of wounded widows. We met a young woman who had been befriended by the Presbyterian Vice President, and who had been helped head to Daystar University. As people kept surfacing, we followed up where we could. There were meetings here, prayer times there...all of which brought us close to dozens of key people. It has all been part of the Ministry of Presence that we believe God has given us.

Almost inevitably, something came from these friendships. Doors opened and opportunities arose. We found ourselves in the middle of Rwanda's grief...with opportunities on all sides to help.

To the world, Rwanda had been known as a place of a kind of environmental tourism. It was a last viable place of the kingdom of certain beasts. It was the world of Diane Fossey and "Gorillas in the Mists."

Now, its reputation is very different. "We are not any worse...any more evil...than other people," one of these young government ministers said to our team in November of 1996. The grief of Rwanda was in his voice. He knew what the world thought: the horrible killing...tribe against tribe, neighbor against neighbor, and family member against relative. How could this all have happened? How could such horror overtake any country?

The young government minister loves his country. He loves his people…Tutsi and Hutu both. He wants to heal the hurt. He wants to rebuild the nation. He wants love to live. He wants civility to mark Rwanda's life. He wants justice done, and he wants people to find each other in respect and cooperation again…or perhaps for the first time, but he lives with a sadness in his soul.

He is young, and the overwhelming task is so great. His own were murdered as they were in most families. He was himself a soldier who now must win by persuasion and by just decision.

The grief of terrible murderous injustice burdens almost every life in Rwanda, but that is only the beginning of the grief. Part of the grief is guilt. Part of it is loss. Part of it is sadness of soul for the whole land. It sits there, unseen, as pain in the heart of a whole people.

8

America's Own Sorrow in the City

Early on, America became a "sending" society, a "going-out" people. This was particularly true in the interests of faith, evangelism, and the telling of the message that had brought its first Europeans to the shores of the American wilderness.

America traded with Europe from the Pilgrims' produce that was sent back to the adventurers who had capitalized their Mayflower voyage. Trade with England grew, as did diplomatic travels to France after the Revolutionary War.

As the churches of Pilgrim tradition became established and pushed west, and were joined by evangelists, pastors, circuit riders, and priests endeavoring to reach the frontier towns and Indians in the wilderness lands before them, the mission turned world wide. The Congregationalists sent young couples to the Sandwich Islands. Adoniram Judson had already gone to Burma, never to return. The American Board of Commissioners to Foreign Missions was formed after the 1810 days of the Haystack Prayer Meeting at Williams College.

The first great worldwide missionary thrust of the churches of America established the tradition of world mission as well as of homeland mission in America. Later in the 19th century the same movement wrought a passion to care about the city, and about the poor who grew as a class even as an industrial society produced a class of new wealth. America had its "robber barons," its "river gods" trading up and down the rivers, its seekers of oil, and developers of steel. Names such as Rockefeller, Carnegie, and Mellon became household names throughout the land.

As the city in England produced desperate poor and a Charles Dickens rose up to cry out against it, America too, had its ills and injustices of the city. These were compounded by the sin of slavery that became such a curse and struggle in the soul of the new nation.

In the mid-19th century, America became the place of vision for the world, where the "tired, poor, and restless masses that yearned to breathe free" aspired to come. The immigrants came from Ireland, Europe, and Scandinavia…just as the Pilgrims and Puritans had come from England. The process began of wave after wave of newcomers getting caught in the ports where they landed. Without funds available to move beyond the places where they had disembarked, they stayed, forming the first ghettos of those cities that were the first homes of every group who came to the new country.

While America had its Harriet Beecher Stowe and her *Uncle Tom's Cabin,* and later its muckrakers such as Sinclair Lewis, poverty grew in America's cities, and in its Appalachian hollows, and on its Indian reservations. Color was a factor. Language made a difference. Strange ways from other countries made transitions difficult. As one wave of immigrants established itself, it became all too easy to look down on and take advantage of those who came after.

Further, too many good people were so interested in building success for themselves that America was unable to develop the kind of care that it needed to have for those poor whom Jesus said we would "always have with us."

So cities now stand, with terrible sores of addiction, moral confusion, and social and economic poverty. People hardly know how to care for themselves, inhabiting places of dirt and grime where buildings and hope are used up, while those of privilege…whose homes are among green lawns, blue pools, and spacious malls far from the sight of these dregs…do everything *not* to see what in many cases they have left behind.

Gibson Winter, in his *Suburban Captivity of the Churches,* challenged many of us in the early 1950's to lead our congregations into the city to care for its people, which we did. The 50's and 60's of the latter 20th century became great decades for churches…as well as for many corporate and community groups…to return into the city to make a difference. The Salvation Army and the Settlement House movement had led the way for doing this in the middle of the 19th Century.

Yet something never became quite right. Good intentions grew and blossomed, and reforming mayors, earnest police departments, and sincere citizens invested themselves and labored to give order to the city. But something persisted in the American city that lived like a kind of grief and sorrow in its soul. It was a sorrow and grief that emptied all too quickly into the will to strike back in revenge…either blindly against the white, successful, isolated, prosperous society, or just as often darkly and unthinkingly against its own neighbors in poverty. Again and again the streets boiled up and burned each other. Crowds smashed and looted stores, but also hurt each other. Madness characterized our cities' streets.

As great movements to fight poverty rose…such as the New Deal and the Fair Deal…new rounds of building started. Houses to churches bloomed in the 1950's, followed by wars in Korea and Vietnam, while protest movements and political programs such as the Great Society gave rise to stark housing attempts stand now almost as city prisons. Drugs, dirt, and despair slink around stairwells, teenagers take their own lives, and schools become hostile gathering places of anger, with guns and knives everywhere.

The rage reaches out onto the highways that criss-cross and circle cities. People are shot for a glance, and police who stop offending motorists are battled for doing their duty. A liberal society trying to be "fair" loses sight of "the right thing," and is all too ready to ignore offenses by people who press the limits, taunt the system, and get away with casting aspersion on those who exercise society's demand for order.

Things always seem to have gone too far before anyone can get hold of what's happened, begin to knit the pieces together, make a reasoned claim for justice and mercy and the possibility for a humane society to be rebuilt. The efforts to bring people together always seem to be a little too late, and a lot too little, for what seems to be needed if the heart is to be healed, and if each human life is to be touched and transformed.

Beginning to Commit as Comrades

American society lived through Rodney King and O.J. Simpson, and justice and truth seemed impossible to establish and isolate and lift up as markers for society. Protest appealing to race seemed to become the order of the day. Adding the dimension of wealth and a particular kind of populist fame made justice all the harder to effect.

Truth mattered little when compared to the shell of now celebrity lawyers at playing on emotion, appealing to prejudice, and calling up the ghosts of a thousand hurts of 300 years. Yet again there are those who say that we must try. These idealists say that human beings share a core as people…a core that can be touched so that seeds of love can be sown, forgiveness can become a new goal, reconciliation is at least a credible vision in a day when so many seem blind, and keeping order alone cannot still the pain that seethes within so many.

So our Center for Reconciliation is also charged by its friends and supporters to go to the cities of home to lay the healing hand that is so welcome in the far country. Perhaps here, however, the cynicism and even the fear are greater. How can anyone know enough and do enough, compared to the focus of government and order that have committed resources and countless lives to "turning it around" in the city?

In Rwanda, the Church is key…the Church that failed and yet is needed. It is needed because it has *access to the people* and a *role* as moral guide. With the hope and prayers that the country of Rwanda might be recovered, we went to the churches, and began with the ministers. These were hurt and wounded ministers, who themselves had suffered deeply and were grieving, but who, in some instances, had fled and not defended the flock…had not "stood in the evil day."

Despite our knowledge of these ministers' pain, we had seen, almost incredulously, the freeing of their burdens. We had seen the healing of people whose grief had bound them as slaves, whose fear had kept them from even their ministry tasks. We knew what God could do! We saw His power work! "I saw Satan fall like lightning from heaven!" my wife had exclaimed in the words of Jesus.

Could any of that work in America? Could the cities of the nation catch even the glimmer of a way, through what God was doing half a world away?

Sitting quietly with one minister at a time, from their service in the center of the city, serving especially the black community, we began to talk about the pain of our own lives, of even our ministries, and of the grief within, carried by *both* of us, white as well as black.

One man said, "I had never claimed as my own the pain of slavery that had so hurt my ancestors." Now, in these latter days, he had begun to recognize what that had been, what it had done to his parents, his grandparents, and his great-grandparents. He was just discovering as a modern man what that terrible injustice really meant to him.

Another, sitting later at the same lunch table, was a bit bemused at the idea of a retreat for black and white together in the midst of the pain of the city we shared. "It will mean nothing unless there is something afterward. Unless there is regularity. Unless there is relationship. Unless somehow, we have a chance to be friends."

Suburban wealth and city poverty are clearly obstacles to weaving anew the "tie that binds." The bridging role is not a happy one. People…even Christian people…of wealth, never do enough. And if they did it all, paid for everything, it would be too much.

How do you still the stirrings of resentment, built on top of the lifetimes and histories of rejection, diminishment, and disrespect that black people, young and old, have experienced for all of their memory? If they fought back, even only in their hearts, at the forces that protect the white and wealthy, how can "the other side" ever be seen, really understood, and appreciated?

The answer has to be "It can't." You cannot live what others have lived. You cannot feel their pain the way they feel it. You can, however, offer *your* pain and *your* experience. You can hold out your heart and appeal to the heart of the other. You can embrace your common humanity, which is deeper than race, higher than poverty, and wider than prejudice.

When that is offered, it is our experience that God does what only He can do. No amount of social experience or intricate arrangement of economics, job opportunities, or gracious living accommodations can do what He does.

God offers the life of His Son Jesus. God offers the cleansing blood of Jesus. God offers His cross, and in the cross of Christ" we glory." What we claim is its power that we know is *mystery*. We stand our ground and offer ourselves for whatever God will choose to do, as both "sides" lay claim to the cross for whatever it can be and do.

Our experience is that people of faith, sitting simply and equally around the cross, open themselves to a power not their own. It is a power very different from any negotiation, any "arbitration," or any "getting to 'yes'" can do, as these actually only lead to a division of the spoils of self-interest.

We have seen God work. We know well how unlikely it sounds. We understand clearly what the wisdom of the world says, and we bank on the foolishness of God. We know from Jesus and from our own experiences that there is power here to heal.

It is our vision that this process of small and quiet retreats can begin to soften hearts toward each other and open lives to the possibility of brotherhood and sisterhood. We believe the "ministry of presence" can create a new atmosphere for a few people. From that, only God knows what can follow.

The vision we propose to the cities of America is our commitment to be comrades.

What It Will Take

We do not know what it will take to make this commitment…perhaps a wild surmise, a radical willingness, a daring to operate no longer at the level of politics and economics but at the level of faith, where we say, "God, *Bible*, and belief is what we have in common. We all love Him. We all preach Him. We all turn to Him. If we dare to risk at any point and start here, let it be at this. Let us dare to try. Let us take our Lord seriously, and each other's intentions seriously, and eventually the authenticity of each other's heart seriously, and let us see what God will do."

In the meantime we will practice a ministry of "presence" to each other…the simple commitment of being there. We will seek forgiveness for our race, our friends, our country, our churches, our Church, and mostly, for ourselves.

Can We Be Healed at Home?

Can we be healed here in America, in this "land of the free and home of the brave?" Is this place…the beginning of so much…incapable of being healed itself? Is "America the beautiful" hopeless?

Our Center, our Reconciliation Team, thinks not. Our experience tells us that God really *is* God and that He can do what is only God's work to do. We can do nothing ourselves except put ourselves in the path of His work.

There can be no answer for people of faith but a "yes" to the possibilities of the healing of America…the healing of America's cities and of the deep rift between rich and poor, black and white, and safe and vulnerable. Our work in the Great Lakes of Africa convinces us of this, because there we have seen God's work.

My 40 years as a parish minister…first among rural hills, then in a city's core, and finally in a suburb of the powerful…convince me by quiet, faithful, year after year experience that people *do* change. White people and black people can be brothers. Rich people *can* humbly care about poor people. Bridges *can* be built across every human chasm there is…between suburb and city, between liberals and conservatives, between sexually straight and gay, between women and men, between Middle Americans and the people of Africa.

We saw relationships build in the "going out" of people across those bridges. We saw miracles happen in the lives of many. We saw human beings learn to give, and learn to live…with love. It was the work of the cross then. It is that central work now.

People of faith do not *need* to follow their culture into isolation, fear, or diminishment of others. We do not need to give way to the least in us, or the worst in us. We *can* reach for the stars. We *can* dare…like Don Quixote…to take on the dragons of the world, allowing our true hearts and honorable faith be present in the mix. The One Who makes all things possible is *here*.

9

Partners in Ministry

Today "partnership" is all the rage…in business enterprises, ministry and mission organizations, and even in pastoral ministry. For over twenty years, young couples in parish ministry have experimented in "co-ministry"…one couple either sharing one job and one salary, or wherever possible, one couple each working a full-time ministry for the church. The key question has been how to divide that ministry, and much has been said about doing it according to a couple's several and separate "gifts."

Clearly the ministry in a parish involves some very public tasks and "up-front," influential, formative, and visible roles. None of these is more public and visible than preaching.

Can this role be divided? Should one preach this Sunday and the other one next? What if one is a *better* preacher than the other…more engaging, more interesting, more dramatic, better weaver of the story of faith, or better Biblical expositor? Or…what if one does teaching and the other preaching? Or, should one do pastoral care and the other administration?

The report of many couples who have tried this type of partnership is that it was *too hard*. It was too easy to be in competition with each other, too bruising of egos, and simply too hard on the marriage itself. The solution for some couples who were able to secure separate calls was to serve separate churches and each do the whole ministry in separate churches.

Husband and Wife

I had never thought of the parish ministry as *not* a partnership with my wife. We have been together in our love for Christ, for the Church, and for people in all of the 40 years that we lived among people of faith as their minister and his wife.

For us at least, it would have been phony to characterize ourselves as co-ministers or "Mr. & Mrs. Minister." There was no doubt in any of the three churches we served that *I* was the minister, or that the church had called *me* to be the minister.

On the other hand, those churches were all intensely interested in my Molly…who she was, her background, education, engagement in church, and most of all, her *faith*. I am sure they all wanted her to help me. They wanted to feel that we saw our life as a partnership in serving Christ.

But they also very much wanted her to be my *wife* and mother to our children, helping them grow up in faith as whole and hopeful young people…and to help me survive the ministry to which they had called *me*.

After 40 years of Arthur being the minister, and Molly being the "helper," it suddenly became very different in our "beyond the pulpit" years! Now we travel together. We do retreats together. We sit in a circle under the cross together. We visit with African friends, we lay plans, we travel the world by air…and the dangerous overland roads of Central Africa by car…together.

I write letters out by hand, and Molly types and changes them. We make speeches together and she cuts out great chunks of what I planned to say. Her gifts and instincts are different from mine. Her thinking is clear and terse with no wasted words. Mine is circuitous and meandering, circling around to make the point.

We are not always as delicate and perceptive and sensitive as we need to be, but our love goes deep, and it has survived much. The gifts of the other are very clear to us, and we both recognize that the call to serve together was not *our* plan…or even our brother Tekle's plan. It was *God's* plan.

This call upon Molly's life…the depth, meaning, and passion of it for her…is wondrous for me to behold. This sweet grandmother…so wise, experienced, and loving with our children and grandchildren…now ministers to broken people the ages of her own children *half a world away*. It is truly wondrous to behold.

In the years I had expected to journey out alone, I find it good for me to go together…to *have* a partner and *be* a partner. It is good to learn from my life-long partner, to work along side her. It is good to moderate our differences, and to be alone together when day is done…even in countries far from home, sometimes in primitive circumstances, and still be friends.

Indeed, it is even good to face uncertainty and perhaps danger, together. We know that the Boeing 747 across the world is not infallible, and that the light Caravelle over the Rift…5000 feet above Lake Victoria…could be tossed about in a minute. The road to Bujumbura is not sure…nor is the return.

As far as God leads us, we will go together. We will share the adventure. We will offer what we are, and what we have together. We may go down together...or more likely, we will go safe with angels together.

It is all new, this partnership in service of Christ our Lord. Each day we learn.

Brothers in Faith

There was, of course, another partnership in this work of reconciliation. The gift to us from the partnership with World Vision was the remarkable man of faith, our dear Ethiopian brother Tekle. He and his family moved to Minnesota, and lived here for the first several years. As our International Program Director, he prepared the way in Rwanda for all three of us go.

It was a gift that God created...black and white, Ethiopia and America, partnering together in the work of reconciliation. Two men...both visionaries, both believers, both leaders...learned to live and work together, after fifteen years of loving and knowing each other from a distance.

Tekle has never ceased to be brother to me. "Our brotherhood is made in heaven," he said. And so it is. We have had differences: He is the internationalist, "the African," and I am the "American" and President of the Pilgrim Center. We've traveled together, and traveled separately, and on some occasions has traveled with Molly while I have come on alone...ahead or behind.

The world, I believe, may ask, "How many partnerships like these are there in the world?" Color and country mean little, we respond. We are different, we know, but we can work and *be* together...because of Christ.

The Partnership Principle

It is that there are many gifts, but "the one spirit." The gifts of another can be honored, because they are needed. It is the way the whole Church, Paul says, comes together and works together as the Body of Christ.

For so many years, leadership in the parish church demanded a lonely life of the preacher/pastor. He or she is the one who takes the risks and takes the hits, leads the way, and gathers others. We are now a network of partners going together, working together, planning together, proclaiming together, and learning together...passing back and forth the lead.

We have a Board of Directors who cares, serves, gives, counsels, and travels out. We also have a vital support staff that believes, shares the vision, and labors long to makes all the "details" work.

The partnership goes many ways, but its witness is oneness. It is unity in Christ. It is the mystery of what Christ does when we give ourselves to Him and let His Spirit work.

We know for sure that it is all a gift.

10

The Ministry as Adventure Worldwide

I had not early on considered myself a "travelin' man." I loved "the face of my parish." I loved going in and out among the people in our first little church there among the foothills of the Berkshires. There the places I wanted to go were up and down South Street, along the way of the "big houses" on North Street, and out along Briar Hill Road to the tarpaper homes of town.

And yet, there had lived in me…longer than I realized…a wanderlust that had made hitchhiking as a preteen-aged boy high adventure. I had learned to love being out on the roads in New England at dawn, with my thumb up and my little satchel with clothes in hand. There was a certain "call" to the open road that I came to love, and an adventure in traveling into the unknown of a new day.

In all the years of parish ministry, I loved the being "settled" in a ministry, as they used to say. I loved having "a" place, and "my" place within that place.

I loved the cycle of the seasons: the beginning of the Church's year in autumn, the coming of Thanksgiving, and the move into the expectant time of Advent. Christmas was always wonderful and mysterious to me, followed by the New Year and Epiphany. I loved Ash Wednesday and the long seeking and penitence of Lent…culminating in Palm Sunday, Maundy Thursday and the Upper Room, Good Friday and the three hours before the cross, and the waiting for the dawn of Easter, when everyone met on the hill in a town park in a rejoicing service held for the whole town. I loved the moving toward Pentecost, with the mystery of tongues and gifts. We even included Memorial Day and Independence Day, and brought them both within the life of the church. Summer had its own style and spirit, a welcome change of pace with concerts on the front lawn, and a standing invitation to the entire town to join us as a Christian community.

I did not live my life to be away from that, or to be away from those people. My joy was to be with them…to go in and out among them, to listen to their hearts, and to help to heal their hurts and remind them where was their hope.

Yet, from the beginning, my call was to mission. It was to sending and being sent. I had the sense that, as *Hebrews* says, the Church has no earthly home. The Church is the Pilgrim company, the journeying people, the people ever moving out in answer to the call to care for the world.

So, I always knew that the Church's life was about leaving nets and the beloved seaside, to follow the Stranger who stood ever on the shores of life, challenging His chosen ones to "come, follow Me, and I will make you fishers of men."

The Long Preparation

As I look back over much of a lifetime…over boyhood, school, athletics, service, and pastoral life through three congregations…I realize that my sense of adventure grew, and "the journey out" came about gradually, step by step.

From the very first day, ministry was an adventure of the heart for me. Facing each day and the unexpected that it might bring was excitement for me.

Again and again, a faithful parish minister is called to be on the front line, in the midst of painful human predicaments, as well as amidst joyful personal celebrations. You are there when crisis comes, when a child dies, and when love fades and divorce comes. In the highest and the lowest times of life, the parish minister is summoned to be there. Out of the stuff of those experiences, he or she speaks publicly, Sunday by Sunday, to the congregation's need, and to the world's need.

The call to the ministry itself began for me in a confrontation with the poor, with one man's deep longing and questioning. Later, through the years work was done always with the knowledge of the poor and the disadvantaged in mind. Safe suburbia itself was a ministry lived on the edge of others' need. Often you merely sent money, but again and again, you went, practicing "presence" in the lives and needs of other people.

In the Berkshires we brought the ones in need to come to live with us "in the country." In the city of Newton, just outside of Boston, we went back and forth to be with the young, the black, and the poor whose friends in faith we tried to be.

More bridges than ever were built in the suburban years. Across two urban cities and many contiguous suburban cities our people and friendship went. We shared the city's turmoil. We served and gave. We fashioned institutions to meet the needs of the young, the newly released prisoners, and kids who were not learning in their schools. We helped with the alcoholic, the aged, the destitute, the prisoner, and the welfare system itself when it ran out of funds.

Even before God's call to Africa came, we had "come our own" in the streets of the city.

After the call came to feed a hungry world, we came home and began city programs of feeding that have never ceased to serve.

The church's mission of course, did not begin with Africa. Already we had a mission presence in the barrios of Mexico, on the barges of Hong Kong, and in the little hospitals of Lien Hip and D'am Pao in Vietnam, through Project Concern. Through HCJB, Navigators, and Wycliffe Bible Translators, we had missionaries in Ecuador, Guatemala, the Philippines, and later in Australia. Campus Crusade for Christ, International Christian Fellowship, Young Life, and Youth for Christ took us out across America. We were in the Navajo nation through Project Concern, and in the hollows of Appalachia.

When the call came to Africa, through World Vision, we were ready. Step by step, God led us, through that great mission organization, to the critical needs of the African people and of the human race.

First it was to the stark physical need of hunger that had become starvation among the Pokot people in northwestern Kenya. There it was up to the great feeding camps of Ethiopia. After that was the valley from where the answers could come...in water resources beneath the land, new agriculture, and a new economy with a road built known as the "Holy Highway." A million seedling trees a year were grown in that valley of Antosokia, and Humbo and Western Abaya provided other valleys for the replication of the process. Finally and surprisingly, in little Mekoy came a church...a gift that God gave, that had never been a part of the program.

Starvation started it all, followed by water resources and agriculture. Then was the new church and faith alive. Later we responded to orphans in Uganda, AIDS in both Uganda and Tanzania, micro enterprises in the village of Lesotho, and a children's center in Soweto. Finally, at the deepest level, are the wounded memories, the anger and fear of the human heart, and the killing and the guilt, of Rwanda and Burundi.

God gave us what we could take. He taught us along the way. The steps were His, until we were back full circle to those pastoral tasks that came to bear where the burdens are invisible, and the heart cries out for healing and for forgiveness, and for the chance the human heart always craves...the chance to live together.

The Going

It seems clearer now than ever that the Christian call is ever to the "going out." The fundamental thrust of the call to follow Jesus, to move out from yourself to the world beyond…first to family and neighbors, and then to the country and the world.

"Go ye into all the world!" was Jesus' watchword. "I have other sheep in other pastures," He said. "I have other cities to which I must go. Preach the gospel to everyone, everywhere."

In some way, it was inevitable. His was a *carrying* movement, a *bearing* movement…the carrying of Good News, the bearing of a message to "tell it out abroad that Jesus Christ is Lord, to the glory of God the Father!" It is meant to be full of the joy of a wonderful experience of one's life having been touched…if not transformed…and of rushing to tell it to whomever will listen.

In that understanding, I suppose the parish church becomes the basic receiving unit of the Christian enterprise, the first reception center, the first safe harbor, the first welcoming arms of a fellowship of love, joy, thought, proclamation, teaching and training, and preparing for service and witness. Longing, struggling, and wrestling in soul, the wanderer is led somehow, probably miraculously, to the parish church, the Sunday-go-to-meeting company of believers, who receive these souls from the world and draw them in.

There, in the early stages of life within the Christian community, their hands are taken, and they are of all things loved, and then led and gradually taught to know Jesus, and to hear the glad Good News that they are loved by God and forgiven through the cross of Jesus. As they feel their way, they receive by grace, through an in-filling of the Spirit, certain "gifts" that enable they themselves to do ministry. The gifts may build on their natural abilities, or they may be essentially mystical gifts given to them from "beyond" themselves. They are in the best sense "super natural" gifts. They are not simply "natural," but they are *more* than natural.

By such gifts coming into the life of the Christian community through these new converts and learners, the Church "body" is built up. The Church as truly the "Body of Christ," the working company…of not just listeners or "attendees," but actual "ministers" who are serving *believers*…the Church grows strong and is prepared for the primary call, which is to *go out*. Individual Christians go out, and his or her church body as a whole, "goes out."

While the church has a "place," a base, a gathering spot for its joyous life of worship and praying, singing, working, teaching, and preaching, goes on, that place is primarily a mission station. It is the base for operations. It is, most uniquely, the institution of sending.

Of course, people are called to care for that base…to keep it alive and vital, and see to that central task. There needs to be regular worship, usually some sort of building, or some identifiable place of gathering. There are people who need to operate there…a pastor or "shepherd" to that ever changing, growing "flock" of God. All other roles will function there too, as a teacher if needed, an administrator, and healer.

He or she may be paid, and may be surrounded by various others, including "lay" ministers who share similar gifts, and who, by practicing those gifts, enable the whole work of the church to grow.

For some of us, the question has been, when do we physically, literally *go*? Can a settled pastor go…and come back? Does each one whose primary task is caring for and teaching the flock of God, *have to* "go?" Or, is it understood that the "going" is to be only done by they whose gifts and jobs suggest it…that is, the "evangelist," or perhaps the "apostle?"

Two models became important for me. One was the ministry in the 18th century of John Wesley of England, who had tried to be a missionary in America, and failed, and then was spiritually transformed by an experience with the Living Christ at a home study gathering in a certain "House on Aldersgate Street."

He was filled with such a passion, such a Spirit power in his preaching, that he became a threat to his fellow clergy, and he was no longer welcome to preach in the churches of England. Since their doors had been closed to him, Wesley, his brother Charles, and his friend George Whitefield took to the streets, or rather to the fields. Wesley became famous for his "field-preaching" when 10,000 people might gather to watch and hear him preach.

When challenged about why he was preaching outside the ordered parish system of the English Church of that time, John Wesley's answer was the simple response has passed down to many of us who are his descendants in the ministry: "THE WORLD IS MY PARISH."

It is also so for me. It has come to be that after 40 years of settled parish ministry, with the last dozen of them moving in an ebb and flow of going out and coming back to the parish I loved. I now can say that for me, literally and fully, "the world is my parish." It is my place of proclamation and pastoral care, my place of dealing with people, healing and helping them, and loving and serving them. It is not in a local company of Christians whose life is ordered by the weekly and seasonal round of Sunday worship and Easter and Christmas seasons, but rather it is people "out there." It is people in the center city, people in remote areas of Africa and India…people of all kinds in all places.

I am not their pastor, but I am their *friend*. I counsel and care, teach and preach, heal and advise. I do the work of the ministry on a world scale…certainly not to the scale of Billy Graham's millions. It is to a few at a time, scattered in places as far apart as the cities of Vijayawada, Nagercoil, Kulpahar, Delhi, Bombay in India; Kiwawa, Nairobi, Kitale, and the Mathare Valley in Kenya; Mekoy, Humbo, Abaya, Karuba, and Addis Ababa in Ethiopia; Johannesburg, Capetown, Soweto, and Mpuma Langa in South Africa; Kampala, Karengeti, and Masaka in Uganda; Bukova in western Tanzania; Goma in Congo; and Kigali, Rwanda, and Bujumbura, Burundi. All of these places are my home now, in the home of my heart. They are my parish, my far-flung parish.

The other model is the retired President of the United States, Jimmy Carter. In his senior years that could so easily have been his golfing years, he goes out…with hammer and saw…to build Habitat for Humanity houses in Eagle Butte, South Dakota, in Watts, Los Angeles, and in the Bronx, New York. He goes to Haiti, Ethiopia, and Bosnia to do his work of international negotiation, a political/spiritual mission of reconciliation.

He's my model because he's an old man. He has done his "main" work of service as President, but he is not *done*. He has built up skills and passions, abilities and connections, and he honors them all.

Further, he partners with his wife. He and Rosalind go together, and they are more powerful, more affective, than if each went alone.

"The world is my parish!" It is a new ministry, a new kind of parish…a new *way* of doing ministry. It is God's gift in this day.

The Face of My Parish

Who are they, these new parishioners…so different from those of my former congregations?

Some are the same people. They write long and timely letters, or crisp encouraging ones. One is David, an articulate professional who says, "I write to you, my friend, my teacher, my father, my persistent wrangler, my beloved evangelist…"

Another is Mary Lou on the assembly line, a wistful young woman who calls to say, "Dr. Rouner, I have not seen you in three years. Could I come and talk with you…just about life?"

One is the little high school girl in Starbucks Coffee shop who bounces up and says, "My name is Sarah. I was your last confirmation student. I am here, having a Bible Study with two of my high school friends!"

Jane stops me in the parking lot outside the coffee shop and says, "I've been thinking of you. When my divorced husband died, my unresolved anger at him lost its last chance at forgiveness. Could we meet? Could you help me know what to do?"

But they are not just the company of those old friends and comrades, left from the days when I was once their "official" minister as pastor of their church.

There is the young man in prison, who was never in the church I served, but whom I have visited and who writes to me still.

They are those who still gather on early Wednesday mornings in a local restaurant to read the *Bible* with me and pray for the people of their world who are so close upon their hearts.

They are ministers, scattered across the country, who are glad to meet and share lunch and coffee just so we can talk together about their ministries, and pray for each other.

Some are other peoples' parishioners, yet my friends in distant cities, who have said, "I want to Journey Out with you. I want to go to England's green and pleasant land, to learn the stories of the martyrs of the faith who gave their lives so I might have a faith, a heritage of believing."

Or they write as one who simply says, "I wish to go. I urgently need to go to Africa or South America or somewhere in the Third World to have my heart broken from the vanity and conceit that fills it. I need, as Erik Erickson would say, to have my instrument calibrated."

In a far country, they are the young elders of Kiwawa's church, so long divided, who say, "You are our only real elder who is an older man of experience. You are as pastor to us who care for this flock."

There is the young Pokot lecturer in Nairobi who asks for help to do the work of reconciliation so needing to be done between his Pokot people in western Kenya and their mortal enemies, the Karamoja of Uganda.

They are the members of the small church in Mekoy in northern Ethiopia, who write, "Will you come to the dedication of our church? You are our founding father in faith, and Colonial and your Center are our Mother Church."

In Uganda, it is dear Samson with his street ministry in Kampala, Canon Kibuka in Naugebo, the President's wife, our praying Christian sister, and her secretary, Panina, who say, "Why, of course, you must call me. You are my father!" In that same country they are John and James, mature men who gave years to helping young people of their land through the Boys' Brigade of Uganda.

In grieving Rwanda, it is Kahunga, a pastor who says after our retreat, "I am not afraid any more." Or Jean Pierre, who says, "Oh, if you had come with these simple, quiet healing retreats right after the genocide, Rwanda would be 3/4 of the way to being healed by now." Or Francoise, the "Hutu from the north," who said in a retreat of the staff of the Protestant Council of Rwanda, "I became a Christian as a child. But I was born again, here, tonight."

On and on it goes, and there is no doubt for me where I have been called, and Who has called me. There are "other cities" too for me, and other people who were not of that flock I loved so much, to whom I have needed to go.

If it extends not another day, the authenticating mark of my Lord and His Holy Spirit has been upon it. It has been His work and His call…no doubt.

"Is it to go forever?" My children ask. "Will you never be retired, and stay home, and do what grandparents are supposed to do? Must you always be a minister, always going out? Do you not know when to say 'enough'?"

Maybe I don't. But the ministry was never a "job" for me. It wasn't ever simply a profession. It was a life. It was what you did and who you were. It was all day and every day.

You had a family, dear to your heart. And you took time for them, and served them. You also had a right to rest, and find renewal and refreshment…perhaps somewhere away, from time to time.

But your commitment in life was to His ministry. It could change, but it wasn't meant to simply end. If there were forces that worked to end it for you in one place, it didn't mean it was to be the end of it *all. It could go on.*

God, I am absolutely sure, did not plot the pain and power moves of the few who brought about the end of my parish ministry. I have no doubt that He was there, redeeming it all, and using even the worst of the pain to bring me to something new…a different kind of ministry that would build upon the foundation of the one He had built over so many years. It was, as Principal John Baillie of New College Edinburgh, had called "Divine over-ruling."

So for me, the ministry goes on. It did not end in disaster after 40 years of service. It was born again into a new ministry, an even deeper, wider ministry across the world, and as deep into the heart as you can go…to its core of grief, its most awful guilt, and its most haunting, wounded memory.

Oddly, all that I have left behind and miss…the pulpit and the people…has taken on new wonder, new joy, and even new freedom. Now, in hand with my wife, and with my dear colleagues, comrades, and friends, I am flung out across the world, to places I had never intended to go, and to people I had never dreamed of knowing.

The days go on…and the exciting years. How many of them will there be? How can I possibly tell?

I simply know it is a miracle that I can still *see*. That still I can climb a mountain, row a racing shell, drive a car, and hold a pen and write. I will go as long my body lasts, and I will rejoice in every minute of the journey. I will try, as often as I can, to sing as I go!

And I will invite all who are open, to join me on this wonderful and unexpected Journey Out to the world, in the hope that we may…in these surprising years…do something together to heal its broken heart.

About the Author

Following 40 years of service in parish ministry—at the First Congregational Church of Christ in Williamsburg, Massachusetts; Eliot Church in Newton, Massachusetts; and The Colonial Church of Edina, in Edina, Minnesota—Dr. Arthur A. Rouner, Jr., founded The Pilgrim Center for Reconciliation in 1994.

Based in Edina, Minnesota, the Pilgrim Center is an international outreach ministry dedicated to healing the wounded and broken hearts of individuals and communities.

Initially approached by World Vision in the 1980s to help with African famine relief, Dr. Rouner subsequently expanded his role throughout the continent of Africa, helping to lead efforts for the development of water resources, agriculture, AIDS relief, and orphan assistance. In 1995, World Vision again approached Dr. Rouner, asking him to create and implement a ministry of reconciliation among the grieving survivors of the genocide in the African nations of Rwanda and Burundi. Along with his wife Mary (Molly) Safford Rouner, Dr. Rouner now travels to Africa several times per year, conducting intimate healing retreats with Church, women, and youth leaders.

In *Beyond the Pulpit*, Dr. Rouner shows how God used his 40 years of parish ministry to prepare him for the critical, deeply personal, and highly sensitive ministry of reconciliation to which he was called after leaving the parish.

0-595-30061-8

Made in the USA
Lexington, KY
09 February 2011